C-REACTIVE PROTEIN

C-REACTIVE PROTEIN

Everything You Need to Know About

CRP and Why It's More Important

than Cholesterol to Your Health

SCOTT J. DERON, D.O., FACC

Contemporary Books

Chicago   New York   San Francisco   Lisbon   London   Madrid   Mexico City
Milan   New Delhi   San Juan   Seoul   Singapore   Sydney   Toronto

Library of Congress Cataloging-in-Publication Data

Deron, Scott J.
    C-reactive protein : everything you need to know about crp and why it's more
important than cholesterol to your health / by Scott J. Deron.
        p.   cm.
    Includes bibliographical references and index.
    ISBN 0-07-142642-6
    1. C-reactive protein—Popular works.   I. Title.

QP552.C17 D47   2003
612'.015752—dc21   2003011987

1 2 3 4 5 6 7 8 9 0 AGM/AGM 2 1 0 9 8 7 6 5 4 3

ISBN 0-07-142642-6

Interior design and composition by Robert S. Tinnon Design

McGraw-Hill books are available at special quantity discounts to use as premiums and
sales promotions, or for use in corporate training programs. For more information, please
write to the Director of Special Sales, Professional Publishing, McGraw-Hill, Two Penn
Plaza, New York, NY 10121-2298. Or contact your local bookstore.

This book is printed on acid-free paper.

Dedicated to Patti, my life partner,
with heartfelt love and appreciation, and to
Loren, Nathan, and Shelby,
whose existence reminds me every day to
leave this place better than I found it.

Contents

Acknowledgments

This work exists because of key individuals. My sincere appreciation to John Pino, Mom and Dad for direction, Vince Glielmi for his humor, Bernie Siegel for his compassion, and Mike Jennings for his humanity.

1

What Is C-Reactive Protein?

Stacey left her doctor's office with an overwhelming sense of relief, clutching a slip of paper recording a cholesterol count that was well under normal limits. Her father had died at age forty-five from a heart attack, and—given her fondness for thick milk shakes and double-cheese pizzas—Stacey had been worrying about her own heart health. Now that she had been given the "all clear," she decided to reward herself with a cheeseburger and fries on the way home.

Two weeks later I saw Stacey in the emergency room after she'd had a massive heart attack. The first thing she asked me was, "How could this happen to someone with normal cholesterol levels?"

What Stacey hadn't realized, and what her doctor had failed to point out, is that her cholesterol level revealed only part of the picture of how healthy she was. Too many people don't realize that *half of all heart attacks and strokes occur in people with completely normal cholesterol levels.*

Of course, cholesterol matters; it ranks as one of the heart's primary villains. But now we know a high cholesterol count is not the *only* indication of heart problems. Over the years, scientists have identified at least 250 other heart disease risk factors ranging from obesity to gum disease, but they never found a better indicator of heart health than the levels of good and bad cholesterol in your blood—until now.

Now we know that measuring the level of *inflammation* in your body is even more important than cholesterol level, and the simplest way to assess inflammation is by testing for the concentration of a protein that is released as part of the inflammatory process. This substance is called C-reactive protein (CRP), and it is produced by the liver during episodes of acute inflammation—part of your body's basic emergency response system. In the past

1

three years, there has been mounting evidence that a high CRP level doubles your risk of heart disease and stroke—even if you have low cholesterol and blood pressure.

If you don't know your own CRP levels, you should. Between 25 and 35 million Americans have normal cholesterol levels but above-average levels of inflammation in their cardiovascular system as identified by CRP. This inflammation has a significant impact on heart disease risk. In the following sections, I'll explain why.

INFLAMMATION AND CRP

Studies of more than eighty-five thousand people over the last ten years show that inflammation is always present in the heart's blood vessel walls among heart attack patients with normal or near-normal cholesterol levels. To understand how this happens, let's first look at the role that inflammation plays in the body.

Inflammation is an immune response triggered by infection or injury. When your body's immune cells break down injured and dying tissues to make way for new healthy tissue, it produces redness, heat, and swelling. For example, when you experience a painful swollen bump after banging your head, that's local inflammation at work. When you develop a fever in response to an infection, that's a type of full-body inflammation produced by your immune system to create an unfriendly environment for germs. But sometimes, your body's inflammatory response is *too* intense, and when this happens, it can do more harm than good.

It's clear that atherosclerosis (hardening of the arteries) is an inflammatory disease, although experts aren't sure exactly what it is that triggers the onset of the inflammatory response in the arteries. Experts used to think a heart attack occurred after too much cholesterol built up in the artery walls, hardening into plaques that eventually interfered with blood flow; as blood flow dropped, the heart couldn't get enough oxygen, triggering a heart attack.

While this scenario probably does occur in some cases, many other patients experience something much more dangerous. In these patients, plaques don't build up on the *inside* of artery walls, blocking blood flow; instead, they grow *into* the vessel wall, pushing it outward. Because the artery stays wide open, no blockage will show up on an x-ray. These bulging plaques are small and may seem harmless, but we now know they can be quite deadly because of their potential to become unstable.

Whether the cholesterol plaque is simply blocking an artery or has grown into the wall, pushing it outward, your immune system responds in the same way: it sends armies of special white blood cells to attack the plaque that has accumulated in the artery. All of this immune cell activity alerts the liver to produce CRP, which floods in to help attack the growing piles of dead germs or plaque. As immune cells rush into the artery and inflammation ensues, the process inadvertently creates or worsens plaques on the artery walls, making the plaques increasingly unstable. When attacked in this way by the immune system, the plaque can burst, exposing the material inside to circulating blood. Once exposed to the blood, this material quickly causes clot formation.

Even people with low cholesterol are vulnerable to this inflammatory process because by the time they reach middle age, most people have accumulated at least some plaque buildup in their arteries.

INFECTION AND INFLAMMATION

Because inflammation is so closely linked to infection, researchers for some time have suspected that artery disease may be caused at least in part by an infectious component. It could be that inflammation is triggered by the activity of low-grade, chronic bacterial or viral infections, such as those caused by the herpes simplex virus, the bacterium *Chlamydia pneumoniae*, or the ulcer-causing *Helicobacter pylori*. These microbes may move into the arteries (perhaps by hitching a ride on white blood cells), where they may begin to damage blood vessel walls.

Indeed, some research has indicated that people infected with these germs are at significantly higher risk of heart disease caused by a state of chronic, low-level inflammation aggravated by the continued presence of the microbes. For example, one recent study of more than six hundred patients discovered that those who had been infected with the herpes simplex virus were twice as likely to have had a heart attack than those who weren't exposed to the virus.

It may be that the artery damage is not directly caused by the disease agents, but that the presence of chronic infection elsewhere in the body forces the immune system to constantly produce white blood cells and send inflammatory products into the blood. For example, the inflammatory effects from periodontal disease (a chronic bacterial infection of the gums) sends bacterial by-products flooding into the bloodstream, which triggers the liver to produce artery-inflaming CRP, contributing to heart attacks or strokes.

CRP: SYMPTOM OR VILLAIN?

Previous research clearly showed that CRP can be a useful warning sign of heart disease risk, but until recently, experts didn't know if the protein was just an innocent bystander or if it might somehow be involved in causing heart problems itself. Now we know it does both.

A study published in early 2003 at the University of California, Davis, found that CRP is a key culprit that can actually inflame the arteries itself, triggering the formation of clots and plaque that lead to heart attacks and strokes. CRP can even cause cells in the arteries to produce higher levels of a crucial enzyme known to interfere with clot breakdown. This is why a high CRP level can accurately predict future heart problems, even among otherwise low-risk patients, such as those who don't smoke and who have normal cholesterol and blood pressure, no family history of heart disease, and no diabetes. CRP has multiple, independent effects that cause heart disease.

Whether CRP itself causes heart disease or is simply a symptom of heart problems, what matters is finding out whether you have high levels of inflammation—because that's a sure sign that all may not be well with your cardiovascular system. And bear in mind that other well-established heart disease risk factors, such as obesity, lack of exercise, smoking, and high blood pressure, all are known to increase inflammation and CRP levels. (In fact, fat cells constantly produce CRP, which might explain why being overweight is so bad for the heart.)

That's why it's important to include your CRP level in your overall risk score, which your doctor can use to assess the total impact of many different factors on your heart health. While it might not be possible to figure out exactly *why* your CRP levels are rising, you should regard a high CRP level as a warning that your risk factors are not being adequately controlled.

HISTORY OF CRP

Since the 1930s, physicians have used CRP levels to measure inflammation in the body, because they knew that CRP levels are high in patients with inflammatory diseases such as rheumatoid arthritis. Yet while scientists have been aware of this protein's existence for more than seventy years, they have only recently begun to understand its role in cardiovascular disease.

Back in the 1930s, it was fairly rare to develop heart problems caused by artery blockage, but just a few years later, American doctors were suddenly presented with an alarming epidemic of blocked arteries. Perplexed by this massive increase in heart disease, scientists set up the now-famous Framingham Heart Study in 1948 to find the reasons why.

This enormous research trial of 5,209 men and women between the ages of thirty and sixty-two resulted in more than a thousand scientific publications that broadened and clarified our knowledge of heart disease. It was the Framingham data that confirmed the tremendous impact of cholesterol: the more you had, the more likely you'd develop a heart attack or stroke.

Yet as time passed, it became clear that cholesterol couldn't be the only culprit, because about half of all patients who developed strokes or heart attacks had perfectly normal cholesterol levels. Up to that point, doctors thought artery blocks were simply a buildup of cholesterol debris, much the way hard-water lime deposits build up inside a copper pipe, narrowing and eventually blocking water flow. But if so many patients with low cholesterol were developing heart disease anyway, doctors reasoned that something else must be going wrong deep within the arteries of the heart.

Eventually, pathologists discovered that the development of heart disease required far more complex explanations than a simple buildup of cholesterol-laden plaque. As scientists examined diseased arteries, they found that next to relatively normal areas of blood vessel were very well defined areas of abnormality filled with white blood cells—the hallmark of inflammation. Scientists realized that somehow arteries were becoming inflamed, and this seemed to be intricately involved in the development of blocked arteries leading to heart disease and stroke.

CRP Studies

It has been known for decades that patients who come into the hospital with problems of blood flow to an organ have elevation of CRP. The first description of CRP elevation in patients with unstable angina was reported in 1990 by Dr. B. C. Berk and colleagues.

Reporting in the *New England Journal of Medicine* four years later, Dr. G. Liuzzo and colleagues demonstrated that CRP levels of patients with unstable angina were useful in predicting their long-term outcome—the higher the

CRP level, the more unfavorable the outcome. Next, a 1997 study then demonstrated the ability of CRP to predict heart attacks in patients who were suffering from angina.

Several groundbreaking studies have been reported by Paul Ridker, M. D., director of the Center for Cardiovascular Disease Prevention at Brigham and Women's Hospital in Boston. A 1997 report in the *New England Journal of Medicine* demonstrated CRP levels are elevated many years before a heart attack or stroke. The men in this study with the highest levels of CRP had a three-fold increase in their risk of heart attack and a twofold increase in their risk of stroke compared with men who had lower levels. Elevated levels were found to predict heart attacks as many as six to eight years in advance.

Building on a growing body of evidence, Dr. Ridker and colleagues sought to establish how CRP compared to other measureable substances in the blood-stream to predict future heart attack. In a 2000 *New England Journal of Medicine* report, researchers measured a variety of substances known to be present during active inflammation in more than 28,000 women. These included CRP, interleukin-6, homocysteine, and amyloid A. Total cholesterol and low-density lipoprotein (LDL) levels were also measured. Of the twelve different substances measured, CRP proved to be the strongest predictor of future cardiac events.

Dr. Ridker went on to publish an extremely important article in the *New England Journal of Medicine* in 2002 where CRP and LDL cholesterol levels of 28,263 women were measured. Over the ensuing eight years, researchers looked for heart attacks, strokes, death, or blocked arteries. The results were consistent with previous information—the higher a woman's CRP level or LDL cholesterol level, the greater the risk of a potentially life-threatening event. Importantly, the study found that women with the highest LDL and CRP levels were at the greatest risk, and those with the lowest LDL and CRP levels had the least risk.

The big surprise was that women with high CRP and low LDL levels had *more* heart problems than those with low CRP and high LDL levels.

These very important observations in thousands of individuals confirms CRP's place as the best predictor of future life-threatening events.

In a subanalysis of the above study, 188 women developed diabetes during the eight year followup period. Interestingly, these same individuals had significantly high levels of CRP. Those with the highest CRP levels were nearly sixteen times more likely to develop diabetes.

Many doctors believe that inflammation plays a key role in the development of diabetes, and these data support the idea and add to the relative importance of knowing your CRP level.

The latest evidence on CRP doesn't change the current guidelines about treating high cholesterol, which remains a very important independent risk factor for heart disease. Indeed, those patients with high levels of both CRP and cholesterol are at even higher risks for heart disease or strokes than people who have either of these risk factors alone.

Even if you're getting regular CRP tests, you should still monitor your cholesterol levels and other risk factors such as blood pressure, weight, and lifestyle habits. Even physicians who rely on CRP testing say they use screening in conjunction with—not as a replacement for—cholesterol testing.

Measuring both cholesterol and CRP provides a better indicator of your risk, because the two measurements look at heart problems from different angles. While a cholesterol test can tell you whether or not plaque is forming in your arteries, an hs-CRP test can tell you how likely it is that the plaque will rupture.

While we know that folks with high cholesterol are at high risk for heart disease, we now know that people with low cholesterol aren't necessarily healthy either. In fact, people with very low cholesterol may still be at very high risk for heart disease. Remember Dr. Ridker's study, where people with *low* LDL cholesterol and *high* CRP levels had *more* heart problems than people with *high* LDL cholesterol and *low* CRP. This suggests that testing for CRP is an extremely important way to identify people at risk for heart problems.

What experts don't yet know is whether lowering CRP levels reduces heart attacks and deaths. Those studies have not yet been done, but a large trial involving fifteen thousand people began in January 2003 to help answer that question.

CRP AND PROGNOSIS

In addition to predicting heart attacks and strokes, high levels of CRP also correspond to a lower survival rate once these problems occur. Recent studies also suggest that higher levels of CRP may increase the risk that an artery will reclose after it's been opened by balloon angioplasty.

Although high levels of CRP can reveal a heart attack in the making, it's not foolproof. If you're fighting a cold or coming down with the flu, your CRP levels can spike as much as ten times normal levels. CRP levels also rise in response to inflammation caused by other diseases, such as arthritis and lupus, which I'll discuss in more detail in Chapter 3.

IN THE NEXT CHAPTER

Now that you have a basic understanding of the inflammatory process under-lying artery disease and the role CRP plays in this scenario, it's time to decide if you should have a CRP test. In the next chapter, I'll discuss current CRP guidelines, including who may benefit the most from testing and what you need to know before having a CRP test.

2

Should You Be Tested?

Jim was an attorney and a patient of mine who walked into my office with a time bomb ticking away in his chest. He smoked countless packs of cigarettes a day, ate too much of the wrong things, and had a family pedigree littered with heart disease. His own daughter—a critical care nurse—constantly begged him to start living a healthier life, but to no avail. Jim's cholesterol was normal, so he thought he was fine. Nothing anyone said seemed to motivate him to change until the day he found out that his CRP levels were sky-high. For some reason, that tangible symbol of his potentially clogged, inflamed arteries seemed to wake him up the way nothing else had. When he stopped by my office a few months later, I couldn't believe the change: he'd quit smoking and had actually lost 20 pounds! That CRP test is a great motivator. Time and again, I've seen poor test results turn folks into cardiovascular saints almost overnight.

To me, the greatest attribute of the CRP test may be its ability to motivate people to start doing something about their health. Because CRP is the only inflammatory marker that can reliably indicate heart health, I usually order a CRP test together with a blood fat profile to help predict a patient's risk of a heart attack. (A blood fat profile is a group of tests that reveal a patient's levels of triglycerides, cholesterol, and lipoproteins.) Without CRP testing, patients with moderate cholesterol levels who are still at risk of a heart attack might not be identified—until they end up in the emergency room.

Some doctors also find periodic CRP testing a valuable tool to help them decide how to treat patients already diagnosed with coronary disease. In patients already known to have atherosclerosis, rising CRP levels can indicate that a plaque is growing or a clot is becoming unstable. In these cases, an elevated CRP reading might warrant more aggressive anti-inflammatory or lipid-lowering therapy.

Questions about how exactly to interpret borderline or fluctuating CRP findings have made universal testing somewhat controversial, but I believe that a CRP test and a blood fat profile should be part of everyone's basic health file, beginning at about age eighteen. After all, if heart disease is going to take out half of the population—and remember, one out of two Americans ultimately die of heart disease—then we should be using every screening tool at our disposal to diagnose this problem. And the sooner the better.

Most studies clearly show that the higher your CRP levels, the higher your risk of having a heart attack. In fact, the risk for heart attack in people whose CRP levels fall in the upper third is twice that of those whose CRP is in the lower third. Recent studies also found an association between sudden cardiac death, peripheral arterial disease, and CRP levels. (However, not all of the established cardiovascular risk factors were controlled for in this study, so the true independent association between CRP and new cardiovascular events hasn't yet been established.)

Remember that the liver produces more CRP whenever there is inflammation somewhere in the body. If CRP levels are high, this means a part of your body is inflamed. This information can be important in diagnosing infections and inflammatory conditions or evaluating the effectiveness of certain treatments.

THE A TO Z OF CRP

Standard tests for CRP have been used for the past seventy years as a way of assessing patients with inflammatory conditions such as rheumatic fever or rheumatoid arthritis. The standard CRP test worked well enough for identifying general inflammation in the body, but it wasn't sensitive enough to detect the low levels of inflammation related to heart disease risk. It wasn't possible to detect this type of low-level chronic inflammation until the development of the highly sensitive CRP test (called the hs-CRP test), which has replaced the standard CRP test for heart disease evaluation. Although the standard CRP test and the hs-CRP test both measure the same molecule in the blood, the high-sensitivity test is the only one that can detect the extremely low level of inflammation linked to early heart disease.

The hs-CRP test is a simple and inexpensive blood test that in a few minutes can help doctors identify previously undetected heart attack and stroke risks in patients for whom inflammation, rather than cholesterol, may be the key factor. High levels of CRP can accurately predict future heart problems even among otherwise low-risk patients, such as nonsmokers with no family history of heart disease, no diabetes, and normal cholesterol and blood pressure.

The test was approved for evaluating inflammation by the U.S. Food and Drug Administration (FDA) in 2001, and it's now moving into widespread use. It's now available at labs and many doctors' offices, and it's covered by most insurance companies. It usually costs between $15 and $25, although some labs have been known to charge as much as $150.

WHO SHOULD TAKE THE TEST?

Because the hs-CRP test is still a new way of assessing heart health, doctors don't all agree on who should be tested. Nevertheless, many doctors are using the test to measure a person's risk for acute coronary syndrome (clogged blood vessels around the heart). The hs-CRP test is usually ordered as one of several assessments used to put together a cardiovascular risk profile, often along with lipid (fat) tests, such as the various measurements of cholesterol and triglycerides. Many experts believe that the best way to predict heart disease risk is to combine a good marker for inflammation (such as CRP) with the ratio of total cholesterol to high-density lipoprotein (HDL)—the good cholesterol. Recent studies also have shown that the hs-CRP test may be useful in identifying risk in symptom-free individuals as well as in people who have symptoms of chest pain.

In an attempt to come up with some national guidelines on the test, the American Heart Association (AHA) and the U.S. Centers for Disease Control and Prevention (CDC) recently published a joint scientific statement advising that the hs-CRP test may be appropriate only for people at "intermediate risk" of heart disease, but not for those at either end of the risk continuum. Intermediate risk means the patient has a few risk factors for heart disease, such as borderline high cholesterol levels, a sedentary lifestyle, obesity, smoking, a strong family history of heart disease, or a poor diet. Doctors expect intermediate-risk patients to have a 10 to 20 percent risk of having a heart attack within ten years, based on such factors as age, high cholesterol, and high blood pressure. For these people, according to the AHA, the hs-CRP test can help predict a heart attack or stroke and help direct further evaluation and therapy. The AHA also recommended an hs-CRP test if a doctor needs more information before prescribing diagnostic imaging or exercise testing, for example, or to decide whether to prescribe certain treatments, such as drugs.

The new guidelines, which appeared in the January 28, 2003, issue of the journal *Circulation*, try to strike a balance between those who believe every adult should get a CRP test and those who reject it completely because they fear it will draw attention away from cholesterol levels. Yet while the recommendations are considered by many doctors to be extremely conservative, the category of intermediate risk is still quite large, encompassing an estimated 40 percent of U.S. adults—nearly 100 million Americans.

According to the AHA, if, after looking at all your risk factors, your cardiovascular risk score is low (which means the possibility of developing cardiovascular disease is less than 10 percent in ten years), you don't need to take the hs-CRP test right now. Young patients without any other risk factors would probably not be put on treatment even if inflammation were found. And if you're at high risk for heart attacks or stroke or you've already got heart disease or had a stroke, you should be under a doctor's intensive treatment no matter what your CRP levels are. The AHA felt that because high-risk people would be automatically given aggressive treatment, such as blood thinners and cholesterol medications, knowing their CRP levels would not be necessary. The AHA wanted the new rules to focus on identifying those people in the middle range whose treatment and behavior should change.

Frankly, I think the panel's recommendations are too cautious. Obviously, people at very high risk already know they have a problem. But it's the individuals we now consider low risk that I'm concerned about. Ignoring them omits a whole lot of people who might benefit from the test. The conservative guidelines are intended to keep medical costs down and protect patients from false alarms, but if we don't test enough patients, we're missing the opportunity to motivate people to make positive health changes.

As the debate continues, more and more of my patients are coming into my office asking about their CRP levels, spurred on by media coverage of the new studies and medical guidelines. People today are much more willing to take responsibility for their own heart health, and this test helps them take another step in that direction.

WHERE TO GET THE TEST

If you're interested in learning your CRP levels, the first step is to discuss your concerns with your family doctor or cardiologist, and ask if he or she rec-

---

Are You at Risk?

To decide whether you should take the hs-CRP test, ask yourself the following questions:

- Is my cholesterol high (240 milligrams per deciliter [mg/dl] or more) or borderline high (200 to 239 mg/dl)?
- Is my LDL cholesterol above 130 mg/dl?
- Has an immediate family member (mother, father, brother, sister) had heart trouble due to cardiovascular disease at a young age?
- Do I have diabetes?
- Do I have gum disease?
- Do I rarely exercise?
- Do I smoke?
- Am I overweight?

If you answered "no" to each of these questions, you exercise regularly, and you eat a well-balanced diet, you can probably assume that you're not at risk. Even one "yes," however, significantly increases your risk for a heart attack or stroke. An hs-CRP test can help you and your doctor determine if medication or a change of lifestyle is necessary.

---

ommends testing your levels. If you are at even mild risk for heart problems, your doctor should be willing to order the test for you. (Remember to ask for the high-sensitivity version of the CRP test—the hs-CRP test.)

Because CRP levels are linked with periodontal gum disease, some experts believe that patients will be offered CRP testing in their dentist's office in the near future.

IF YOU HAVE A PROBLEM GETTING THE TEST

You can have your CRP levels tested even if your doctor isn't interested in ordering the test or your insurer won't pay for it. In the past, a doctor's order was required before any lab would perform a blood test, but that's not the case today. If your doctor balks at ordering the test or you simply want testing without going through a doctor, direct-access testing (DAT) is now available for those who want to monitor their own health or for those who do not see a health care provider on a regular basis—as long as you're willing to pay for the test yourself. (Direct-access testing companies require up-front payment, since insurance and Medicare won't cover the service because the test wasn't ordered by a doctor.) Also known as patient-authorized testing or direct lab access, DAT is the direct result of the growing sophistication of health-conscious Americans eager to play a more active part in their own health care.

With direct-access testing, results are sent directly to the customer ordering the test. And while the lab won't send results to your physician, you're still encouraged to share them with your health care provider. In most cases, labs provide for physician overview of abnormal results.

You can find direct lab access companies online. For example, Healthtests Direct (health-tests-direct.com) offers the hs-CRP test to anyone in the United States (except California residents). Although the company is headquartered in Costa Mesa, California, they can arrange for blood testing in your hometown. After calling the website's phone number and providing your zip code, the company will tell you the closest lab where you can have your blood drawn. The company will then take credit card payment information (the lab won't accept payment). After getting your payment information, the service faxes a special authorization form to your local lab, which will then proceed with the blood test. After your blood is taken and analyzed, confidential results can then either be e-mailed, faxed, or airmailed to you twenty-four to forty-eight hours after the test was performed.

TESTING PROCEDURE

If you're scheduled for a CRP test, do not eat or drink anything for twelve hours before the procedure. Blood will be drawn from a vein, usually from the inside of your elbow or the back of your hand. Once the blood has been collected, the needle is removed, and the puncture site is covered to stop any bleeding.

Because the hs-CRP test is really testing for the presence of inflammation in your body, be sure to tell your doctor or the lab about any recent medical events that may have raised your CRP levels, such as an injury or wound, any infections, or general inflammation from conditions such as arthritis or lupus. In fact, many other factors may interfere with the accuracy of a CRP test:

- *Diet* You should be advised not to eat or drink anything for twelve hours prior to testing. High-fat foods may influence the test.
- *Pregnancy* Women in the last half of the pregnancy cycle will have some CRP in their blood.
- *Stress* Periods of psychological stress can mildly increase CRP levels.
- *Intrauterine devices (IUDs)* These birth control devices can sometimes cause inflammation, which will mildly increase CRP levels.
- *Statins* These cholesterol-reducing medications, which are often considered a first line of treatment for patients with high cholesterol, will reduce CRP levels.
- *Corticosteroids and anti-inflammatory medications (ibuprofen)* These drugs can interfere with or lessen the inflammatory response, which would lower CRP levels.
- *Birth control pills* These medications may result in a false positive (in other words, the test results would suggest that inflammation is present when it actually is not).

HOW OFTEN TO TEST

In cases of suspected heart disease, doctors use the hs-CRP test as a diagnostic tool, so most patients won't need regular testing. However, regular CRP tests can be used to monitor the progress of treatments aimed at reducing chronic inflammation, because as inflammation decreases, so do CRP levels. Many doctors test most patients once a year while screening patients every six months who have several risk factors or have shown high levels of CRP.

WHO SHOULDN'T TAKE THE TEST

Because inflammation is common in patients with multiple medical problems, experts say that CRP testing should be limited to healthy outpatients. If you do have a huge CRP spike (such as a level that jumps from 2 to 13, for example), you can probably dismiss it as the result of inflammation from an injury or some other condition. (Certain parasitic diseases, such as malaria, will also boost CRP levels, for example.)

CRP Results

The lab should provide an explanation of your test results, but here's a quick overview according to the AHA guidelines:

- *Less than 1 milligram per liter (mg/L):* You have a low risk of developing cardiovascular disease.
- *Between 1 and 3 mg/L:* You are at average risk.
- *More than 3 mg/L:* You are at high risk for developing cardiovascular disease.
- *More than 10 mg/L:* If after repeated testing you have persistently unexplained, markedly elevated hs-CRP at this level, other tests should be considered to exclude non-heart-related causes of inflammation.

People with inflammatory diseases, such as rheumatoid arthritis, should not have their hs-CRP levels measured because their results can't be considered in the context of heart disease. The CRP levels for these patients would be too high for the hs-CRP test to measure meaningfully.

FLUCTUATING LEVELS: WHAT DOES IT MEAN?

Unfortunately, physicians disagree about exactly what small changes in CRP levels mean. This is why the AHA guidelines suggest averaging two measurements obtained two weeks apart for baseline measurement. Some experts believe that substantial low-level fluctuation in repeated CRP tests can indicate a problem. For example, some say that if a patient's CRP level of 1.8 suddenly jumps to 3, it indicates a significantly higher risk for heart disease. Other researchers claim that such a rise can be accounted for by normal variation in CRP levels, which some research suggests may vary as much as 30 percent from one reading to the next.

In other words, most doctors aren't sure what a shift in CRP level from 3 to 3.9 really means in terms of a patient's risk level. If a patient's levels seem highly variable, some experts recommend measuring the level every two to three months to eliminate some of the variability. If an infection is causing a false positive, measuring in a month or two should give the levels time to return to normal.

IF YOUR CRP IS HIGH

While fluctuating levels may be puzzling, a high level of CRP in your blood, together with other diagnostic test results, may send a clear warning of impending heart problems. If your test reveals elevated levels of CRP in your blood, this means that one or more parts of your body are inflamed for some reason. Unfortunately, a CRP test cannot determine the location of inflammation or its cause, which is why the test is often used in conjunction with other diagnostic tests to confirm a diagnosis related to infection or inflammation.

Studies indicate that increased levels of CRP can be present many years before coronary disease sets in. Even if your test results are at the high end of "normal," this test can give you advance warning that a heart problem may develop at some point in your life. You can use this finding as the impetus to make some important health changes in your life! Because there is also a connection between high CRP levels and traditional risk factors, such as smoking, obesity, high blood fats, diabetes, and high blood pressure, knowing your CRP level can help motivate you to stop smoking, get more exercise, lower your blood pressure, lose weight, and eat a heart-healthy diet—no matter what your cholesterol level. In addition, your doctor may want to discuss with you the wisdom of taking cholesterol-lowering drugs called statins, because these also seem to fight inflammation.

Remember that people who seem healthy but who have hs-CRP levels in the highest one-fourth of test results have two to four times the risk of developing blocked arteries, compared with those in the lowest quarter. A few conditions (including diabetes, glucose intolerance, and high blood pressure, all of which are independent risk factors for heart disease) each may cause a mild increase in your CRP levels. And temporary events, such as infection and injury, can cause CRP levels to spike by a factor of one hundred or more.

Many doctors believe that the hs-CRP screening test should be primarily used to accurately assess at-risk populations. Even if you have normal cholesterol but high levels of CRP, I'd recommend an aggressive course of treatment to help you reduce your risk of heart attack, stroke, and other heart diseases. Later in this book, I'll discuss how to do this—by eating right, getting exercise and losing weight (if necessary), and easing stress. If your CRP and/or cholesterol levels are still high after several months of lifestyle changes, it might be time to think of medications to lower these levels, beginning with aspirin and ending with cholesterol-lowering statin drugs.

IN THE NEXT CHAPTER

While CRP has gotten lots of publicity for its usefulness in predicting heart disease and its possible role in causing some blockages, we've known for a long time that it's also elevated in the presence of all sorts of inflammatory diseases. In the next chapter, you'll learn about other conditions linked to high CRP, including arthritis, cancer, diabetes—and possibly even Alzheimer's disease.

3

C-Reactive Protein and Other Diseases

Today we know that a high level of C-reactive protein in the blood is a good marker for heart disease risk. But this is just the latest application of a test we've been using for years to identify a wide range of other inflammatory problems in the body. Normal, healthy people don't have high levels of CRP in the blood, so if your CRP levels begin to increase, something is amiss.

While slightly elevated levels of CRP are linked to incipient heart problems, an extremely high level of CRP may indicate any number of other disorders. These include inflammatory conditions, such as rheumatoid arthritis, rheumatic fever, and lupus; infections, such as herpes, tuberculosis, and pneumococcal pneumonia; and a number of other diseases, including diabetes and cancer. Many of these conditions may cause such significant inflammation that CRP levels may rise as much as one hundred times above normal. There are other, more tantalizing hints that CRP could also be a marker for Alzheimer's, which many researchers have always suspected might have an inflammatory component.

USING THE CRP TEST

In patients with chronic inflammatory diseases (such as some forms of arthritis, autoimmune diseases, or inflammatory bowel disease) the CRP test is used to assess how active the inflammation is. Once a diagnosis has been established, CRP may be used to monitor the patient's response to therapy, since CRP levels drop fairly quickly as inflammation diminishes. Repeated CRP tests can assess whether treatment of an inflammatory disease or infection has been effective.

19

Because CRP levels rise in the presence of infection, doctors can use the test to monitor patients at risk for infection (such as after surgery). The incredibly high CRP level that may occur after surgery may be one reason why some patients who were not considered at high risk for heart disease suddenly experience a heart attack after surgery.

The test can also be of some use in differentiating between bacterial and viral infections. A very high CRP (above 100 mg/L) is more likely to occur in bacterial rather than viral infection, and a normal CRP is unlikely in the presence of bacterial infection. However, intermediate CRP levels (between 10 and 50 mg/L) may be seen in both bacterial and viral conditions.

This kind of testing is especially important when immunosuppressant drugs are being given, since the possiblity of infection is always present. Infections easily monitored by CRP levels include meningitis and infections of the pelvis, kidneys, and heart. Serial CRP measurements are an important addition to the use of temperature charts, since CRP levels are not affected by drug treatments or attempts to lower fever.

There are limits to its usefulness in other conditions, however, since CRP tests aren't specific enough to diagnose a particular disease. For example, a higher-than-normal CRP level can't differentiate between arthritis and lupus. But high levels are a powerful marker of infection and inflammation that can alert medical professionals to the fact that further testing and treatment may be necessary.

Although CRP is the best measure of inflammation within the body, doctors can also use another test to monitor inflammation—the erythrocyte sedimentation rate (ESR). Both ESR and CRP can provide similar information about the presence of inflammation, but because CRP levels appear to be more sensitive to inflammation, it's far more useful to physicians. The CRP test is also more precise and quicker to perform than the ESR test. However, ESR measurements remain helpful in certain clinical situations, such as monitoring Hodgkin's disease.

STROKES

Previous studies have demonstrated an association between CRP levels and the risk of stroke, but most of these studies have looked at patients with many other risk factors for stroke, so it was hard to measure the impact of each individual factor. A new study in the April 2003 issue of the journal *Circulation* carefully differentiates among different risk factors and still finds that CRP plays a role in the development of at least some strokes. The study tested 259 men who had already had at least one stroke and 1,348 men with no stroke history. All of these study participants had had their CRP levels measured twenty years earlier, when the volunteers had been forty-eight to seventy years of age. The researchers studied the relationship between these baseline CRP levels and the subsequent incidence of strokes.

Scientists found that within ten to fifteen years of CRP testing, the men with the highest blood levels of CRP experienced a nearly fourfold increase in the incidence of stroke. Among the men with no history of high blood pressure or diabetes, high CRP levels were associated with a nearly twofold increase in the incidence of stroke. Among men who had the highest CRP levels at or before fifty-five years of age, the incidence of stroke was about three times that of their same-age peers with the lowest CRP levels. Finally, among nonsmokers with the highest CRP levels, the incidence of stroke was nearly six times as great when compared with the nonsmokers with the lowest CRP levels. Only men who smoked, had high blood pressure, had diabetes, or were over fifty-five years of age had no increase in the incidence of stroke with elevated CRP levels.

These results strongly suggest that a high blood concentration of CRP is by itself a significant risk factor for stroke and heart disease, at least in middle-aged men. Among men with other risk factors for stroke (such as age, high blood pressure, diabetes, or smoking), the elevated CRP levels were not significant.

DENTAL DISEASE

For the past several years, one impressive research study after another has strengthened our conviction that there is a link between periodontal disease (a severe form of gingivitis, or gum disease) and heart attacks. At first doctors were baffled as to why an infection in your gums would have such a serious effect on your heart. But as the theory of the inflammatory underpinnings of cardiovascular disease became better accepted, it all started to make sense. When researchers began finding elevated CRP levels in patients with gum disease who subsequently had heart attacks, it began to look as if the oral bacteria were a prime suspect. Now we know that high levels of CRP may be the primary reason why gum disease is a risk factor for cardiovascular disease. In fact, periodontal disease is now so closely linked to high levels of CRP and heart problems, that dentists may soon be offering CRP tests as part of their preventive dental care.

According to current theory, as periodontal disease worsens, oral bacteria pour into the bloodstream, triggering the liver to pump out proteins such as CRP that inflame arteries, eventually triggering the formation of lethal blood clots that in turn lead to heart attack or stroke. So strong are the research findings that researchers now believe the presence of periodontal disease increases the risk of a second heart attack in people with a history of heart disease.

These beliefs are bolstered by a study showing that heart attack survivors who suffer advanced gum disease have significantly higher levels of CRP than such patients without gum disease. According to researchers at the University of North Carolina at Chapel Hill, not only did the heart attack patients with periodontal disease have higher levels of CRP than those without gum disease, but CRP levels were directly related to the severity of the gum disease: the more severe the gum disease, the higher the CRP. Researchers hope that by treating severe gum disease in people who have had heart attacks, they might be able to reduce these patients' CRP levels and their risk of another heart attack.

In similar research, scientists at the State University of New York (SUNY) at Buffalo found that after adjusting for other factors known to be associated with high CRP levels (age, body mass index, and smoking), among the fifty people with advanced periodontal disease, 38 percent had high CRP levels. Furthermore, those patients infected with the bacteria that cause periodontal disease had the highest levels of CRP.

RHEUMATIC FEVER

Rheumatic fever is characterized by the inflammation of many connective tissues throughout the body, particularly in the heart, joints, brain, and spinal cord. The condition is a complication of an untreated strep throat and usually occurs in children between five and fifteen years of age. Today it is a rare complication in the United States; before the development of antibiotics, it had been much more common. Although experts are still unsure what the underlying mechanism is, many believe the disease is mediated by the immune system.

Because rheumatic fever causes a distinctive spike in a patient's CRP levels, a series of CRP tests can help monitor how the disease is progressing and how well a patient is responding to treatment.

RHEUMATOID ARTHRITIS

This disease, which is caused by a misguided immune system's attack on the body's joints, is marked by high CRP levels in addition to inflammation, pain, stiffness, and swollen joints and internal organs. Now researchers think that the inflammation so typical in this disease could also spill over and negatively influence the heart. For example, women with rheumatoid arthritis are twice as likely to have a heart attack as those without the chronic condition, according to a new analysis of findings from the Nurses' Health Study. And women in the study who had rheumatoid arthritis for more than ten years had triple the heart attack risk of women without the inflammatory immune system disorder.

The Nurses' Health Study, which began in 1976, includes 114,342 women (527 of whom developed rheumatoid arthritis during the course of the study); 3,622 had heart attacks. Researchers also found that women with rheumatoid arthritis were older, smoked slightly more, exercised less, and were more likely to have a parent who suffered a heart attack before age sixty than those without the disease.

While previous studies have documented a connection between rheumatoid arthritis and heart disease, this reanalysis is the largest study so far to uncover such a link and the first study to assess healthy people rather than severely ill patients. Although scientists have understood a great deal about what causes rheumatoid arthritis, researchers had never been sure why it had been linked to heart problems. Now experts believe the link between rheumatoid arthritis and cardiovascular disease may be the inflammation that underlies both conditions.

LUPUS

Systemic lupus erythematosus (SLE) is an autoimmune disorder in which the body produces antibodies against its own tissues, causing inflammation of the skin, joints, and organs. Normally, your immune system defends your body against infection. But in SLE and other autoimmune diseases, these defenses are turned against the body as the immune cells produce antibodies against the body's own blood cells, organs, and tissues. These antibodies induce the immune cells to attack the affected systems, producing chronic disease. Scientists don't fully understand the cause of autoimmune diseases, but many suspect that it occurs after infection with a microbe that resembles particular proteins in the body. These proteins are later mistaken for the invading germ and wrongly targeted for attack. SLE may also be caused by certain drugs; in such cases, the disease is usually reversible, subsiding when the medication is stopped.

The disease affects nine times as many women as men and may occur at any age, although it strikes most often between the ages of ten and fifty years. Symptoms vary widely and characteristically wax and wane. In the beginning, only one organ system may be involved, but more organs may be targeted later.

Lupus can be a very challenging disease to diagnose and requires extensive testing of blood, immunological factors, and urine. Although doctors would expect to see a spike in CRP levels in autoimmune conditions, CRP levels rarely increase very much in lupus. In fact, this tendency in the presence of obvious inflammation is one way doctors can diagnose the condition. ESR does tend to increase in lupus patients, however.

Moreover, in conditions such as lupus, where it can be hard to tell the difference between a worsening of the disease and a severe infection, an increase in the CRP above typical levels for a particular patient may provide a valuable clue to the presence of infection.

CANCER

Although doctors don't typically think of cancer as an inflammatory or infectious disease, research is beginning to highlight some instances in which elevated CRP levels are linked to survival rate in some forms of this disease. In fact, in patients with some types of advanced cancer, the presence of a bodywide inflammatory response (as measured by CRP) and the strength of that response may predict a patient's chances of survival. (In general, the higher the levels of CRP, the poorer the prognosis.)

CRP's role as a predictor of survival has been documented in multiple myeloma, melanoma (a type of skin cancer), lymphoma, sarcoma, and cancer of the ovaries, kidney, pancreas, and gastrointestinal system. In several recent studies, high levels of CRP before surgery for colorectal cancer indicated how malignant a tumor was and what the prognosis would eventually be. In at least one study of CRP and squamous cell carcinoma of the esophagus, the appearance of CRP in malignant cells was linked to a significantly worse prognosis.

DIABETES

Disorders of blood sugar, including insulin resistance, metabolic syndrome, and diabetes, all increase the risk of coronary artery disease. Now there is increasing evidence that type 2 diabetes may be related to inflammation and increased levels of CRP. Moreover, high levels of CRP can predict the development of type 2 diabetes.

One recent study demonstrates that CRP prompts cells in the arteries to produce higher levels of an enzyme that interfere with the breakdown of blood clots, causing lesions in the arteries that ultimately lead to the formation of plaque and more blood clots. The enzyme (PAI-1) is also a strong risk marker for heart disease, especially in diabetics.

In another important discovery, this study shows that when there is a lot of sugar in the blood (as would occur in diabetics), CRP is especially active in stimulating PAI-1. This is why the effect of CRP is especially acute for patients with diabetes.

Research continues to uncover links between sites of inflammation in the body and the onset of disease. A new study reporting such a link to diabetes in women was published in the November 2002 issue of *Diabetes Care.* Experts have known that obese women are at higher risk for heart disease and stroke because of an overall low-grade inflammation provoked by excess weight. In the study of 729 women and 515 men over a six-year period, researchers noted that compared to men, women had higher concentrations of CRP, a higher body mass index, a larger waist circumference, and higher insulin levels (insulin resistance). Women also had a comparatively higher incidence of metabolic syndrome. (Having two or more of the following risk factors constitutes metabolic syndrome X: obesity, high levels of LDL cholesterol and triglycerides, high blood pressure, and type 2 diabetes.)

In the study, higher CRP levels in women were associated with the onset of metabolic syndrome and also with the development of diabetes. No such association was found in the male subjects. The researchers suspected this was because CRP is a stronger marker in fatty tissue in women and that the process of inflammation lowers the protective properties of estrogen.

ALZHEIMER'S DISEASE

The cause, diagnosis, and cure of Alzheimer's disease is so elusive and the ramifications of the disease so horrifying that researchers are frantically searching for any clues that could shed more light on this condition. Because many researchers are accumulating evidence that Alzheimer's might be, at least in part, an inflammatory disease, some scientists have suspected that CRP levels might be raised in patients with the condition.

It is therefore not terribly surprising that elevated CRP levels have been found in patients with Alzheimer's disease. In fact, in one recent study, patients with the highest CRP levels were three times more likely to develop Alzheimer's during a twenty-five-year follow-up. Even more intriguing, the higher the CRP level at the start of the study, the higher the patient's risk of ultimately developing Alzheimer's disease.

BIRTH CONTROL PILLS

For quite some time, researchers have been exploring the link between estrogen levels and CRP. Earlier studies had reported the presence of elevated CRP levels in more than half of women using the first-generation combined or sequential oral contraceptives of the 1960s.

There have been conflicting reports about birth control pills, estrogen, and cardiovascular risk. On the one hand, combination birth control pills with lower-dose estrogen carry significantly less risk of cardiovascular problems compared to the older combined formulations with higher doses of estrogen. On the other hand, the current generation of progestins appears less safe than earlier formulations as far as blood clotting is concerned. Moreover, recent studies have associated current birth control pill use with risks for stroke and heart attack. This means there is still some risk to your heart if you take birth control pills.

Checking CRP levels might provide clues as to why this might be so. In at least one previously published study, researchers noted higher levels of CRP in more than half of women using the first generation combined or sequential birth control pills of the 1960s. In a more recent study, CRP levels were two times higher among women who used birth control pills, no matter what their diet or menstrual cycle phase. The results from this research and past studies suggest that estrogenic hormones significantly affect inflammation in the body, but scientists do not yet know what these changes mean.

From another intriguing study, it appears that the estrogen patch may be better for women's hearts than estrogen pills, since researchers found that the pill increases CRP levels, but the patch does not. The three-part study, published in the April 2003 *Journal of the American College of Cardiology*, looked at whether various forms of estrogen replacement therapy raised blood levels of CRP. In the study, twenty-one postmenopausal women were given estrogen therapy by pills and patches, combined with placebo. Each woman took each of three possible combinations: estrogen pills and placebo patches, placebo pills and estrogen patches, and placebo in both the pills and the patches. They used each combination for eight weeks, and each woman's response to one combination could be compared with her own responses to the other two combinations. Blood samples showed that the CRP increased to an average of almost twice their baseline levels when the women took oral estrogen replacement, but not when they were on the estrogen patch. It appeared that the oral estrogen therapy overstimulated the liver to produce CRP, which could in turn be harmful to the heart. In addition to doubling the CRP levels, the estrogen pills suppressed the levels of insulin-like growth factors, proteins that can provide anti-inflammatory and disease prevention benefits.

IN THE NEXT CHAPTER

Now that you've learned something about what CRP is and how it may be both a marker and a cause of heart problems, it's time to learn more about how to minimize your risk of developing cardiovascular diseases. In the next chapter, we'll discuss all sorts of heart-healthy diets, and you'll see how a healthy diet can help you lower your levels of CRP and, ultimately, your risk of heart disease.

4

Diet: Eat, Drink, and Be Wary

Roger came into my office one day complaining of being so short of breath that even taking a shower was a big effort. This wasn't a tough problem to diagnose—Roger was 5 feet 7 inches tall and weighed 379 pounds; he'd been gaining about 15 pounds a year ever since high school. When I asked him what strategies he'd used to deal with this problem, he looked at me blankly and responded, "*What* problem?"

With the extra weight he carried, the strain on his heart was obvious; yet he seemed to have no idea that his diet was endangering his heart and interfering with his breathing. I showed Roger how to calculate his ideal body weight: For men, 106 pounds is the ideal weight for someone who is 5 feet tall; you then add 6 pounds for every inch over 5 feet. (Women start with 100 pounds at 5 feet and add 5 pounds per inch thereafter.) When Roger calculated his own ideal body weight at 148, he realized his heart and lungs were basically doing the work for two people. I explained to him how short of breath I get when I carry an 80-pound bag of salt to the water softener in the basement. Essentially, Roger was carrying an incredible 231-pound "bag of rock salt" he could never put down.

Right there in my office, we set some weight goals for Roger to work toward and discussed healthy diet and exercise strategies to achieve them. Today Roger is making great progress. All he needed was to understand how devastating that extra weight was to his body—plus a little nudge in the right direction. On follow-up visits, Roger proudly tells me how much smaller his "bag of rock salt" is getting every month. In fact, he credits that analogy with much of his success. While I doubt that the simple analogy itself is responsible for his continued success, it may well have lit the fuse.

As I explained to Roger, a healthy diet is crucial if you want to lower your CRP and cholesterol levels and keep your cardiovascular system healthy. In fact, diet is so important that the American Heart Association (AHA) regards obesity as a major risk factor for heart disease.

The good news is that diet is something you can control. If you're overweight, you'll need to lose weight as soon as possible, because obesity heightens the inflammatory process and increases your CRP level. Even gaining an extra 10 or 20 pounds can substantially boost those inflammatory proteins.

WHICH DIET IS BEST?

The grapefruit diet . . . high carbohydrate . . . high protein . . . the rice diet—which should you choose to shed pounds? There are as many plans out there as there are pounds to lose, but what I tell my patients is that all those fad diets don't make it any easier to lose weight and keep it off.

The best diet to help lower both cholesterol and CRP levels is quite simple: eat plenty of fish, whole grains, fruits, and vegetables, and limit saturated fat and cholesterol. Increasing your daily consumption of four to five servings of fruits and vegetables to eight to ten servings while cutting back on saturated and trans fats can lower your heart attack risk by 15 percent and your stroke risk by 27 percent. (Trans fat comes from adding hydrogen to vegetable oil, which partially hydrogenates it. It tends to increase blood cholesterol levels.) Healthy food habits can help you reduce four risk factors for heart attack and stroke: high blood cholesterol, high blood pressure, high CRP levels, and excess body weight.

The American Heart Association Eating Plan for Healthy Americans is based on similar dietary guidelines:

- Eat a variety of fruits and vegetables (eight to ten servings per day).
- Eat a variety of grain products, including whole grains (six or more servings per a day).
- Eat fish at least twice a week (particularly fatty fish, such as salmon).
- Include fat-free and low-fat milk products, legumes (beans), skinless poultry, and lean meats.
- Choose fats and oils with 2 grams or less saturated fat per tablespoon (liquid and tub margarines, and canola, corn, safflower, soybean, and olive oils).

At the same time, you should limit foods high in calories or low in nutrition, including foods with a lot of added sugar, such as soft drinks and candy, and those that are high in saturated fat, trans fat, or cholesterol (whole milk products, fatty meats, tropical oils, partially hydrogenated vegetable oils, and egg yolks).

Remember that every meal doesn't have to meet all the guidelines, but it's important to apply the guidelines to your overall eating pattern over a period of several days. If you can do that, not only will you improve the health of your heart you'll also reduce the risk of other chronic health problems, such as adult-onset (type 2) diabetes, osteoporosis, and some types of cancer.

Alternatively, you may want to try the DASH diet (discussed later), which has been effective in helping people lower their blood pressure and improve their heart health.

INCREASE FRUITS AND VEGETABLES

It's fine for doctors to advise you to eat six to eight servings of fruits and vegetables. Actually swallowing that much healthy food may seem impossible. Try gradual substitutions: choose a medium apple instead of four shortbread cookies, and you'll save 80 calories. And remember, if you need to add a hefty number of fruits and vegetables to your diet, make a gradual change so as not to disrupt your gastrointestinal system with all that extra fiber. If you're used to eating one or two vegetables a day, add just one more serving at lunch and another at dinner at first. If you don't eat fruit now or you only drink juice at breakfast, add one serving to your meals or eat a fruit or vegetable as a snack. Once your system adapts, add another serving until you reach the recommended six to eight servings.

WATCH THOSE PORTION SIZES

There's been a lot of publicity lately about huge portion sizes; indeed, they tend to be far too large in the United States.

Check food labels for portion sizes. You may be surprised to see how small they really are. When one of my patients wanted a quick lunch, she'd microwave a can of cheese ravioli. When she checked the label one day, she was amazed to see that the can actually contained *two* servings. Take a quick look at the nutrition label on your morning cereal box and check out the serving size. Typical cereals list a serving size of ¼ cup. If you pour out your usual serving size and measure it, you may find that you're eating two or three times the recommended amount on the label. Now check out the label on a 20-ounce container of soda. If you glance at the nutrition label, you may feel good about the fairly low number of calories per serving. But if you look closer, you'll see that a 20-ounce soda is supposed to provide 2.5 or more servings. If you're drinking the whole thing, your calorie count is much higher than you thought it was.

Between 1977 and 1996, U.S. portion sizes ballooned, not only at fast-food restaurants but also at conventional restaurants and home kitchens. In my opinion, "supersizing" is a critical health problem today. For example, back in the 1950s, one popular fast-food chain offered just one size of an order of french fries; today that same size is labeled "small," and it's now one-third the weight of the largest size.

Ethnic foods also got supersized when they hit Western shores. One study found that the American croissant is bigger and contains 100 more calories than one in France. The original bagel, baked by Jewish bakers from Poland, weighed 1½ ounces and contained 116 calories; today's American version is about three times the size and calories. In Mexico, a quesadilla is a 5-inch tortilla with about 540 calories and 32 grams of fat, but the American version is typically 10 inches with more than 1,200 calories and 70 grams of fat.

Now, if you're going to go out and run a marathon, these huge portion sizes might not be so bad. But very few of us downsize our meal portions as our activity level drops. In fact, 67 percent of Americans usually eat everything or almost everything on their plates, no matter what, according to a 2001 survey by the American Institute for Cancer Research.

Keep all this in mind the next time you drive up to a fast-food restaurant and that electronic voice asks you if you want to "supersize" those fries or "biggie size" the soda. If you're cooking at home, it's even easier to downsize: Try making a 3-ounce hamburger instead of a 6-ounce version, and add ½ cup serving each of carrots and spinach to the sandwich (you'll save more than 200 calories). Or, instead of preparing a 5-ounce fried chicken breast, make a stir-fry with a whisper of olive oil and just 2 ounces of chicken, along with a few cups of fresh raw vegetables. You'll save at least 50 calories.

HOW MANY CALORIES A DAY?

Speaking of calories, remember that you should balance the number of calories you eat with the number you use each day. To find that number, multiply your body weight in pounds by 15 (if you're active). This means that if you weigh 200 pounds, you expend about 3,000 calories in an average day ($200 \times 15 = 3,000$). If you're a couch potato, multiply your weight by 13 to find the calories you expend.

Now, if your body is burning up 2,000 calories a day and you eat 2,000 calories a day, you'll maintain your weight. If you cut back your food intake to 1,200 calories and you're still burning 2,000 calories, you'll lose weight. But if you burn 2,000 calories and you consume 5,000 calories, you'll gain weight.

To lose just 1 pound, you must eliminate 3,500 calories (either through diet or exercise). So if you ordinarily need 2,000 calories per day to maintain your weight, and if you maintain your exercise level, you would need to eat 500 fewer calories a day to lose a pound in one week. If you hate dieting, you'd need to work out long or hard enough to burn off those 500 calories (about 45 minutes of vigorous exercise) to lose the same pound of weight.

The trick is to get enough exercise to keep fit and to balance the calories you burn with the calories you eat. Walk or do other activities for at least 30 minutes on most days. To lose weight, you'll need to get enough activity to use up more calories than you eat every day. And remember: consuming an extra 100 calories a day beyond your needs can lead to a weight gain of 10 pounds a year.

It's a fact that being overweight increases your CRP levels, because body fat promotes inflammation. Fat cells produce large amounts of CRP, interleukin-6, and interleukin-2 (interleukin is a substance that stimulates the liver to produce CRP). All three are powerful inflammation triggers. This may be part of the reason why being overweight increases your risk of diabetes, heart disease, and other disorders.

Luckily, the opposite is also true: losing weight will lower your CRP levels. Eating fewer refined carbohydrates and high-sugar foods, taking natural vitamin E supplements, getting moderate exercise, and losing weight can significantly lower CRP levels. Taking a vitamin E supplement alone can reduce CRP levels by up to 30 to 50 percent.

A recent Vermont study of 61 obese women who lost an average of 33 pounds in one year found that CRP levels dropped by almost a third. Although the women reduced abdominal fat by more than a third, their total body fat loss was a better predictor of CRP drops than abdominal fat loss. The key appeared to be losing fat, since the loss of muscle mass was not related to the change in CRP. In fact, what scientists are now finding is that losing fat is the best predictor of CRP changes. Losing weight not only leads to a decrease in CRP, but also carries additional benefits, such as increased sensitivity to insulin, which is known to help prevent heart disease.

Unfortunately, experts aren't sure *how much* fat you've got to lose to significantly lower your CRP levels. One previous study found that a 6-pound loss had no effect; instead, experts believe it is between 6.6 and 33 pounds.

CUT THE FAT!

For people without coronary heart disease, diabetes, or high LDL cholesterol, total fat intake should be 30 percent of total calories or less; saturated fat should be less than 10 percent of total calories; and cholesterol should be less than 300 milligrams a day. Saturated fats, found in animal products (such as bacon and beef), raise cholesterol levels, as do the trans fats found primarily in processed foods.

Trans fats can be found in corn, safflower, sunflower, and soybean oils and are especially prevalent in fast foods. (Canola and olive oil do not contain trans fat.) Butter naturally contains about 5 percent trans fat; margarine contains between 10 and 27 percent trans fat; and shortening contains the most. Fast foods are often cooked in shortening with a high trans fat concentration (french fries often contain up to 38 percent trans fat). Other major sources of trans fat include commercially baked cookies and crackers prepared with vegetable shortening.

Try to limit your saturated fat intake to less than 10 percent of your total calories. To meet this goal, you don't need to drive yourself crazy. Just make sure that all your food choices over a week's time average less than 30 percent of your calories from fat. If you're eating 3,000 calories a day, then you should only be getting 900 calories from fat. You'll be happy to know that most food labels spell out precisely how many calories come from fat, along with fat grams. Therefore, the can of cheese ravioli we mentioned earlier has 60 fat calories.

If you went to Burger King for lunch and chose a Double Whopper with Cheese (1,150 calories, 33 fat grams), a king size order of fries (600 calories,

30 fat grams) and a large milk shake (1,200 calories, 42 fat grams), you'd be getting 2,950 calories and 945 calories from fat. (These figures are from the Center for Science in the Public Interest.) If you consider that 2,500 calories a day is a healthy goal, you've already exceeded your daily calorie limit in one fast-food meal.

The AHA recommends that consumers limit the amount of harmful fats they eat by following these tips:

- Use naturally occurring, unhydrogenated oil such as canola oil or olive oil.
- Use processed foods made with unhydrogenated oil rather than hydrogenated oil or saturated fat.
- Use margarine instead of butter, selecting soft (liquid or tub) margarines with no more than 2 grams of saturated fat per tablespoon and with liquid vegetable oil as the first ingredient.
- Limit foods high in trans fats (french fries, doughnuts, cookies, and crackers, for example).
- Limit your daily intake of fats and oils to about 5 to 8 teaspoons, which will help you avoid excessive amounts of trans fats.

You Do the Math!

Okay, so you should limit your daily calories from fat to 30 percent. But what if all you know is how many grams of fat are in that burger?* It's easy. If your giant fast-food burger has 1,024 calories and 76 grams of fat , here's what you do:

1. Multiply the number of grams of fat by 9 (the number of calories per gram of fat): $9 \times 76 = 684$ calories.
2. Divide by the total number of calories and multiply by 100 to get the percentage: $684 \div 1,024 \times 100 = 0.67$, and $0.67 = 67$ percent. Voila! This means that 67 percent of the calories from the burger comes from fat.

*Information on fat grams is usually available at fast-food restaurants, either posted in a public area or included on menus or handouts. And fat grams are always included on food labels.

Healthy Fats

We used to think that *all* fats were "bad" fats, but now we know that there are some good fats in the world. Foods high in omega-3 fatty acids can significantly lower your risk of death from heart disease, according to the AHA. Omega-3 fatty acids make the blood less likely to form clots that could block the arteries, and they protect against irregular heartbeats that cause sudden cardiac death. Olive and canola oils are excellent sources of omega-3 fatty acids. People who eat mostly olive oil have lower levels of fat and cholesterol in their blood and a lower risk of clogged arteries. In addition, olive oil seems to lower the "bad" (LDL) cholesterol while raising the level of the "good" (HDL) cholesterol.

To get enough of these healthy fats, try to eat an ounce of nuts three to five times a week and fatty fish twice a week. (Fatty fish include mackerel, lake trout, herring, sardines, albacore tuna, and salmon, which are also high in two kinds of omega-3 fatty acids, eicosapentaenoic acid (EPA) and docosahexaenoic acid (DHA). If you have high triglycerides, you may need 2 to 4 grams of EPA and DHA per day provided as a supplement, according to the AHA. Even the 1-gram-per-day-dose recommended for patients with existing cardiovascular disease may be more than you can get in your diet alone. In this case, you should ask your doctor about taking supplements to reduce heart disease risk. *However, anyone taking more than 3 grams of omega-3 fatty acids from supplements should do so only under a physician's care. The FDA has noted that high intakes of these supplements could cause excessive bleeding in some people.*

Other sources of "good fat" include avocados (high in monounsaturated fats), and plant sources of omega-3, such as tofu and other forms of soybeans, canola, walnuts, and flaxseed. All of these plant sources contain alpha-linolenic acid (LNA), a less potent kind of omega-3 fatty acid.

WHOLE GRAINS

Heart-healthy recommendations include eating six servings of whole grains a day. In one recent study, women who ate two or more servings of whole grains a day had a 30 percent lower risk of heart disease than those who ate three or fewer servings a week. "One serving" of whole grains equals half a cup of high-fiber cereal, brown rice, barley, millet, or whole-wheat pasta.

Fish Alert

Eating large amounts of fish is not necessarily a good idea for everyone. Children and pregnant or nursing women may be at increased risk of exposure to excessive mercury from fish. But these people are usually at low risk for heart disease. Thus, avoiding potentially contaminated fish is a higher priority for these groups. However, for middle-aged and older men and postmenopausal women, the benefits of eating fish far outweigh the risks within the established guidelines.

LEGUMES

Legumes are vegetables (such as beans and peas) that contain heart-healthy fiber as well as antioxidant-rich plant chemicals, and they're also low in blood-clogging saturated fat. Legumes include all types of beans (kidney, fava, navy, bush, string, and lima), soybeans, peas (including chickpeas), and peanuts. If you can manage to eat just half a cup a day, you can block fat absorption and lower blood cholesterol. Legumes are also a good source of folate, which can help lower high levels of homocysteine (Remember, high homocysteine levels can be associated with an increased risk of developing coronary artery disease.) To get enough beans in your daily diet, try eating bean burritos, black bean soup, vegetarian chili, and lentil soup. Although legumes supply the same amount of calories as grains do, they have four times as much protein. Also, they are low in calories and free of both fat and cholesterol.

DRINK TO YOUR HEALTH

Recent studies have highlighted the fact that alcohol—*in moderation*—has been linked to a lower risk of heart problems, lower blood pressure, and lower levels of CRP. In one study, women who drank in moderation were 78 percent less likely to develop high blood pressure. Moderation is the key, however—no more than one drink a day.

Another study concludes that people who drink between five and seven alcohol-containing drinks a week have lower CRP levels than those who consume little or no alcohol. In this study, researchers at Brigham and Women's Hospital in Boston measured CRP levels in 2,833 men and women. The study appeared in the January 28, 2003 issue of *Circulation*, a journal of the American Heart Association. The findings in this study suggest that one reason moderate drinkers tend to have fewer heart problems than those who don't drink may be the fact that alcohol may have an anti-inflammatory mechanism.

A German study lends support to the theory that moderate consumption of alcohol makes hearts healthier because it reduces artery-harming inflammation. The study also supports the current recommendation that only moderate drinking—one or two drinks a day at most—is beneficial. It finds that the molecular markers of inflammation are reduced by low alcohol intake but go up with heavy intake.

When scientists looked at CRP levels in another study of 1,776 men and women whose alcohol intake varied from none to heavy, they found that nondrinkers and heavy drinkers had higher CRP concentrations than moderate drinkers. The more alcohol, the higher the CRP, especially in men. The lowest CRP levels were associated with people who reported drinking between five and seven drinks per week. Those who didn't drink at all had CRP levels almost double those seen in the moderate drinkers.

A much smaller Dutch study found similar results. In this study, CRP levels declined among a group of middle-aged adults who drank three or four glasses of beer with dinner. CRP levels declined by 35 percent after three weeks of regular beer consumption. The effect was particularly pronounced among those who had started out with higher levels of CRP. Exactly how alcohol reduces CRP levels is not clear.

Many studies have suggested that the heart-healthy benefits of drinking alcohol may be due to wine (especially red wine), grapes, or red grape juice. The best-known effect of alcohol is an increase in HDL ("good") cholesterol. However, since regular physical exercise and weight loss also raise HDL cholesterol, it isn't necessary to drink wine to achieve the same effect. Alcohol also may keep platelets in the blood from sticking together, reducing clot formation and lowering the risk of heart attack or stroke.

Although moderate drinkers do have lower heart disease risk than nondrinkers, drinking higher amounts of alcohol increases the risk of alcoholism, high blood pressure, obesity, stroke, breast cancer, suicide, and accidents. Given these and other risks, the AHA cautions you not to start drinking if you don't already drink alcohol. Since you can get almost all the protective effects of

---

Aspirin and Alcohol

The FDA warns that people who take aspirin regularly (such as those taking daily aspirin to lower heart disease risk) *should not drink alcohol*. Heart disease patients should stop drinking and keep taking their aspirin if their doctor prescribed it for their heart condition. Patients should not stop taking aspirin without first talking to their doctor.

---

alcohol in other ways, such as exercising, taking aspirin, or taking statin drugs to lower cholesterol levels, it is not necessary to drink.

If you do drink alcohol, you should have no more than one drink a day if you're a woman or two per day if you're a man. "One drink" means no more than ½ ounce of pure alcohol—either 12 ounces of beer, 4 ounces of wine, 1½ ounces of 80-proof spirits or 1 ounce of 100-proof spirits. The AHA recommends that you consult your doctor about the benefits and risks of consuming alcohol in moderation.

COFFEE AND TEA

Although many experts believe that moderate amounts of regular coffee (no more than about two cups a day) are probably harmless, unfiltered coffee (the type found in espresso, latte, Turkish coffee, and cappuccino) may raise blood cholesterol and homocysteine levels. Swiss scientists studying caffeine's effects in a small group of people reported markedly high blood pressure when occasional coffee drinkers drank a triple espresso, regardless of whether it contained caffeine. Surprisingly, people who drank coffee on a regular basis showed increased stimulation of sympathetic nerve pathways but no increase in blood pressure. The AHA maintains that studies investigating a direct link between caffeine or coffee drinking and coronary heart disease have produced conflicting results. However, experts say that moderate amounts of coffee (one or two cups a day) doesn't appear to be harmful.

Tea, on the other hand, appears to be heart-healthy. Several studies have found that drinking black tea produces both short-term and long-term benefits for patients with coronary artery disease. In one study of several thousand tea drinkers from the Netherlands, researchers found that the more tea a person drank, the less cholesterol built up in the main artery that carries blood from the heart to the entire body. Women who drank more than four cups of tea a day cut their cholesterol buildup by 69 percent. Those consuming two cups a day still cut their chances of clogged arteries 46 percent. For reasons that are not clear, this protective relationship was not as strong in men.

B VITAMINS

Three essential B vitamins—folate, B_6, and B_{12}—help your body recycle the blood chemical homocysteine, preventing it from damaging artery walls. Most people get only half as much folate as they need. And after age fifty, your body doesn't absorb B_{12} as efficiently. A daily dose of fortified breakfast cereal can help you get enough of all of these vitamins.

SALT

Salt can be particularly hard on your heart, especially if you're overweight. One twenty-year study involving almost ten thousand people found the risk of dying from heart disease jumped 61 percent for each additional 1¼ teaspoons of salt eaten daily by overweight people. However, extra salt didn't increase risk for people of normal weight. For this reason, you should limit your salt intake to about 1 teaspoon of salt a day (a daily sodium intake of less than 2,400 milligrams). That may sound like a lot, but think about how much salt is hidden in processed foods. A can of chicken noodle soup has 1,780 milligrams of sodium, and a can of ravioli has 2,120 milligrams. If you ate them both at one meal, you'd have accumulated 3,900 milligrams of sodium—far above your recommended daily level. The FDA estimates that salt contributes between 25 and 50 percent of the sodium in a typical U.S. diet, and estimates by other groups are even higher.

You'd be amazed at the number of foods that contain salt. Although you can detect salt by taste, don't rely on your taste buds exclusively. French fries may have only a quarter of the amount of salt as cherry pie; the sugar in the pie masks the taste of the salt. You'll also find hidden salt in gelatin desserts, milk shakes, cheese, and packaged and frozen dinners. You should limit your intake of processed meats, corned beef, and soy sauce, and remember, artificially softened water also contains high levels of salt.

Rather than throwing away the salt shaker, however, you might simply try to eat eight or more servings of fruits and vegetables a day. Studies show that people who add produce to their diet automatically lower their sodium intake. And fresh fruits and veggies are also high in potassium, which can lower blood pressure.

DASH DIET FOR LIFE

Several studies have shown that blood pressure can be lowered by following the Dietary Approaches to Stop Hypertension (DASH) eating plan and reducing the consumption of salt. The combination of the eating plan and a low-salt approach gives the biggest benefit and may help prevent the development of high blood pressure. The DASH diet recommends a daily sodium consumption of 2,400 milligrams, which is the upper limit of current recommendations by the U.S. National High Blood Pressure Education Program (NHBPEP) and the amount used to figure food labels' Nutrition Facts Daily Value).

The DASH study was sponsored by the National Heart, Lung and Blood Institute and conducted at four medical centers. The study tested nutrients as they occur together in food and showed that blood pressures are reduced with an eating plan low in saturated fat, cholesterol, and total fat and that emphasizes fruits, vegetables, and low-fat dairy foods. The DASH eating plan includes whole-grain products, fish, poultry, and nuts, with lesser amounts of red meat, sweets, and sugary drinks. It is rich in magnesium, potassium, and calcium as well as protein and fiber. The DASH study involved 459 adults with blood pressures less than 160/95; about 27 percent of the participants had high blood pressure.

The DASH study compared three eating plans: one was much like an average American diet, another was a similar plan but with more fruits and vegetables, and the third was the DASH eating plan. All three plans included about 2,400 to 3,000 milligrams of sodium daily. None of the plans was vegetarian or used specialty foods.

Results were dramatic. Both the fruits and vegetables plan and the DASH eating plan reduced blood pressure, but the DASH eating plan had the biggest effect, especially for those with high blood pressure. Furthermore, the blood pressure reductions came fast—within two weeks of starting the plan.

A second study called DASH-Sodium evaluated the effect of a low-salt diet on blood pressure. The DASH-Sodium study included a diet at three sodium levels: a high intake of about 3,300 milligrams a day (the level consumed by many Americans); an intermediate intake of about 2,400 milligrams a day; and a low intake of about 1,500 milligrams a day. Results showed that reducing salt lowered blood pressure for both the 2,400 and 1,500 milligram eating plans. The biggest blood pressure drops occurred for people on the DASH eating plan at the sodium intake of 1,500 milligrams a day. Those with high blood pressure showed the biggest reductions, but those without it also had large decreases. Those on the 1,500-milligram sodium diet as well as those on the DASH eating plan also had fewer headaches. DASH-Sodium shows the importance of lowering salt intake, no matter what you eat, but the biggest benefits come from following the DASH diet and lowering your intake of salt. The DASH eating plan was not designed to promote weight loss, but it's rich in low-calorie foods, such as fruits and vegetables.

The DASH eating plan has more daily servings of fruits, vegetables, and whole-grain foods than you may be used to eating. Since the plan is high in fiber, it can cause bloating and diarrhea. To avoid these problems, gradually increase the amount of fruit, vegetables, and whole-grain foods. Because it is rich in fruits and vegetables, which are naturally lower in salt than many other foods, the DASH eating plan makes it easier to consume less salt.

If you take medication to control high blood pressure, continue taking it. Follow the DASH eating plan, and talk with your doctor about your drug treatment.

Use reduced-sodium or no-salt-added foods and condiments when available. Buy fresh, plain frozen, or canned vegetables with no salt added, and use fresh poultry, fish, and lean meat, rather than canned, smoked, or processed types. Choose ready-to-eat breakfast cereals that are lower in salt. Limit cured foods (such as bacon and ham), foods packed in brine (such as pickles, pickled vegetables, olives, and sauerkraut), and condiments (such as MSG, mustard, horseradish, catsup, barbecue sauce, and even low-salt versions of soy or teriyaki sauce). Flavor foods with herbs, spices, lemon, lime, vinegar, or salt-free seasoning blends. Cook rice, pasta, and hot cereals without salt, and cut back on instant or flavored rice, pasta, and cereal mixes. Cut back on frozen dinners, packaged mixes, canned soups or broths, and salad dressings, because these often have a lot of salt. When possible, rinse canned foods (such as tuna) to remove the salt.

Gradually increase your use of low-fat (1 percent) or fat-free (skim) dairy products to three servings a day. You may want to start by choosing milk with a meal instead of soda, sweetened tea, or alcohol. This will reduce the amount of saturated fat, total fat, cholesterol, and calories you consume. If you have trouble digesting dairy products, try using lactose-free milk or milk with the enzyme lactase added. Whole-grain foods (such as whole-wheat bread or whole-grain cereal) will give you added minerals and fiber. DASH diet snacks include unsalted pretzels or nuts mixed with raisins, graham crackers, low-fat and fat-free yogurt or frozen yogurt, popcorn with no salt or butter, and raw vegetables.

Remember, crash diets may work for a few weeks or months, but as soon as you've lost the weight, the tendency is to go back to your former eating patterns, which got you into trouble in the first place. The DASH plan is a new way of eating healthy for life. Of course, if you slip from the eating plan for a few days, don't let it keep you from reaching your health goals. It's not the end of the world—just get back on track. Everyone slips off a diet now and then. Think about how long it took you to put excess pounds on—and realize that taking it off and *keeping* it off is a long-term process.

Many Americans have an all-or-nothing attitude. Too often we start a drastic diet—one that makes us feel deprived and is doomed to fail. Instead, just try to change one or two things at a time. It's far better to start off slow and succeed!

IN THE NEXT CHAPTER

Now that you've learned how diet can lower your CRP levels and improve your heart health, it's time to discuss another way of lowering these levels—through exercise, one of the best ways to heal your heart.

5

Exercise: Get Moving!

Susan was an overworked, compassionate coronary care unit nurse who could not seem to say no when asked to work extra shifts. With little free time to exercise, the pounds started to add up. Then one day, as she accompanied me on rounds, she was shocked to find a high school classmate who had been hospitalized after a heart attack.

The sight of her old friend—the same age and with the identical weight problem—lying in that bed really shook her up. She saw herself lying in that same bed if she didn't change things—and fast! Hearing me talk to her friend about a new dedication to lifestyle change motivated her to finally do something about her own heart health.

Within two months of instituting a morning exercise routine, she proudly revealed she'd dropped 20 pounds and felt fabulous. She still has trouble saying no to overtime shifts, but she no longer needs six cups of coffee per work shift to get through the day.

Exercise is one of the single most important things you can do to lower your CRP levels, improve your overall health, and keep your heart healthy. Exercise helps control obesity, conditions and strengthens your heart, and can prevent or delay the onset of high blood pressure. In fact, the more you move, the more alive you'll feel—but you don't have to be an Olympic athlete to participate. Research shows that as little as twenty or thirty minutes a few times a week can help.

A number of studies show that people who modify their behavior and start regular exercise after heart attack have better rates of survival and better quality of life. Healthy people—as well as many patients with cardiovascular disease—can improve their exercise performance with training.

CRP AND EXERCISE

According to a CDC study, there is a clear correlation between physical activity and lower levels of CRP in the blood. Experts already knew that exercise can reduce the risk of heart attack, but finding the exercise-CRP link may help scientists understand why. In fact, some studies have found that exercise reduces inflammation by up to 30 percent, and if you manage to lose weight while you exercise, your CRP levels will drop even faster.

Moreover, recent studies have found that men who are physically fit tend to have lower levels of CRP, which could help explain why exercise is so beneficial. It could be that reducing CRP levels in the body is one of the ways that exercise helps reduce a person's risk of heart disease and a host of other cardiovascular problems. During the study, scientists measured fitness and CRP levels in 722 men. To determine how fit each man was, the researchers asked him to walk on a treadmill of increasing incline for as long as he could, reasoning that the better shape a man is in, the longer he could stay on the treadmill. The investigators found that men who were in the best physical shape also tended to have the lowest levels of CRP, while those who were least physically fit were more likely to show the highest levels of CRP. The scientists also discovered that the risk of high CRP levels dropped as a person became more fit, so that those who were the most fit were 83 percent less likely to have high CRP levels than the least fit men. Interestingly, even a slight improvement in physical fitness resulted in a very large drop in CRP levels.

Although the scientists tested only men, they noted that the relationship between CRP and physical activity in women was probably similar, although results might appear less dramatic because of the way hormones influence CRP levels.

Regular aerobic activity increases your capacity for exercise while helping to prevent heart disease. Aerobic exercise also has an independent, modest blood-pressure-lowering effect for certain groups of people with high blood pressure.

HOW EXERCISE CAN HELP

Physical activity helps control your weight by using excess calories that otherwise would be stored as fat. Almost everything you eat has calories, and everything you do uses calories. Even while you're sleeping, you're burning calories, and any extra physical activity you do will use extra calories. By balancing the calories you use in physical activity with the calories you eat, you'll be able to reach a healthy weight. When you eat more calories than you need, your body stores the extra calories as fat, and you gain weight. As your lean muscle mass increases and you drop excess body fat, your resting metabolism rate will improve, so you'll begin burning more calories even when you're not exercising.

Daily physical activity can help prevent heart disease and stroke by strengthening your heart muscle, lowering your blood pressure, raising your HDL ("good") cholesterol and lowering your LDL ("bad") cholesterol, and lowering harmful triglycerides—sometimes within a week or two of beginning an exercise routine. Regular physical activity can lower blood pressure and reduce excessive body weight, which is associated with high blood pressure. (Studies have suggested moderate exercise three times a week is enough to cause a significant drop in blood pressure.) Besides lowering CRP levels and directly improving heart health, physical activity builds healthy bones, muscles, and joints, also reduces feelings of depression and anxiety, improves mood, and promotes a sense of well-being. Studies show that even the most sedentary people can gain significant health benefits if they spend thirty minutes a day exercising.

Millions of Americans suffer from illnesses that can be prevented or alleviated through regular physical activity. Exercise can help reduce or eliminate some of these health conditions and risk factors:

- High blood pressure
- Cigarette smoking: Smokers who exercise vigorously and regularly are more likely to cut down or stop smoking.
- Diabetes: People at their ideal weight are much less likely to develop diabetes in the first place; exercise also may decrease a diabetic patient's insulin requirements.
- Stroke
- Obesity: Exercise can help people lose excess fat or stay at a reasonable weight.
- High triglyceride levels: Physical activity helps reduce triglycerides, which are linked to coronary artery disease.
- Cancer: Research suggests that vigorous exercise may increase breast cancer patient survival and may help to prevent certain types of cancer, including colon and breast cancer.

OTHER BENEFITS

Regular exercise improves the efficiency of the heart so that more oxygen can be used from the blood. Remember that the heart is a muscle, so the more you exercise, the more you'll be training the heart to pump more blood with each beat, easing the heart's workload and slowing your heart rate. The average person who doesn't exercise has a resting heart rate typically between 75 and 85 beats a minute. But after a few weeks of exercise, your heart can become so much more efficient that your resting heart rate could drop by 10 or 20 beats per minute. And the fewer the heartbeats, the less work for your heart.

While exercise has not specifically been shown to lower LDL ("bad") cholesterol, it can quickly increase HDL ("good") cholesterol.

CONSULT YOUR DOCTOR IF . . .

The U.S. Surgeon General has recommended that every man over age forty and every woman over age fifty get a clean bill of health from a doctor before beginning a new exercise regimen. For example, you'll need to know what happens to your blood pressure when you're active. Many people don't realize their blood pressure isn't a static number; it constantly changes, depending on their activities. Your blood pressure might be fine while you're sitting in the doctor's office, but check it while you're on a treadmill and you might find quite a different story.

You also should see your doctor before starting an exercise program if any of these apply to you:

- You have a heart condition or you've had a stroke, and your doctor recommended only medically supervised physical activity.
- You often have pain or pressure in the chest, left neck, shoulder, or arm during or right after exercise, or you've noticed chest discomfort within the last month.
- You get so dizzy you fall or lose consciousness.
- It's hard to catch your breath after mild exertion.
- Your doctor recommended medicine for your blood pressure, a heart condition, or a stroke.

- Your doctor said you have bone, joint, or muscle problems that could be made worse by exercise.
- A doctor has told you that you have high blood pressure.
- You're middle-aged or older and you're not used to physical exercise.

And by the way, contact your doctor immediately if you notice any of the physical symptoms mentioned here after you begin exercising.

WHAT EXERCISE TO CHOOSE

Some activities improve flexibility, some build muscular strength, and some increase endurance. Continuous activities at a regular, even pace that involve the large muscles in your arms or legs while making you breathe hard are considered aerobic activities. They help make your heart stronger and more efficient and use more calories than other activities. Aerobic exercises are particularly helpful in decreasing CRP levels and improving your heart health. The following aerobic activities will increase endurance, and are especially beneficial when done regularly:

- using aerobic equipment (such as a treadmill or stationary bike)
- basketball
- biking
- climbing stairs
- dancing

What's Normal and What's Not

If you're just starting an exercise program, it's completely normal for your heart and breathing to speed up and your body to get warmer while you work out. In the early weeks of training, it's also normal to feel a bit stiff or sore and to be a bit more tired at night. It's not normal to throw up, get dizzy, or faint during or after exercise. And any bone or joint pain or discomfort in the chest, arm, neck, jaw, or upper body should be reported to the doctor right away.

- hiking or walking briskly
- jogging or running
- jumping rope
- racket sports
- rowing
- skating (ice or roller)
- skiing (cross-country or downhill)
- soccer
- swimming

AHA RECOMMENDATIONS

For most healthy people, the AHA recommends some type of vigorous activity for at least thirty minutes on most days of the week. This means that you don't have to head to the gym and bench-press your own weight to lower your CRP levels and improve your health. Moderate-intensity physical activities for thirty minutes or longer on most days provide some benefits. What's important is to include some kind of activity as part of a regular routine.

Moderate-intensity activities may include some of the things you're already doing, such as gardening, housework, walking around the neighborhood, and yard work. By itself, none of these activities would have much effect on your health, but regularly building up thirty minutes of activity over the course of a day can result in substantial health benefits.

Take advantage of any chance to get up and move around. For example, when you drive to work tomorrow, try parking your car a little farther away from the building where you work, and walk the extra distance. When you get to work, walk up the stairs instead of using the elevator. After a few hours, take a break; get up and stretch or walk around. At lunch, try taking a short walk around the block. When you get back home, don't just sit there and play Nintendo with your kids; go outside and play ball or ride bikes together. Rake leaves, mow the lawn, or mulch the flower beds. The point is not to make physical activity an unwelcome chore, but to gently incorporate activity in your daily life, making the most of every opportunity to be active. Too many Americans have an all-or-nothing attitude, believing that if they can't exercise for two hours a day, there's no point in exercising at all. That couldn't be further from the truth.

START SLOWLY

If you're 40 or 50 pounds overweight and the heaviest thing you've lifted lately is the TV remote, you don't want to suddenly jump into an exercise program by pumping iron. While heavy exertion only rarely triggers a heart attack, it's most common among folks who previously have exercised very little. What you want to do is ease into movement very slowly at first. Since you can't see the condition of your arteries by looking in a mirror, you should go to the doctor for a physical before starting an exercise program. Beginning slowly will allow you to become physically fit without straining your body; once you're in better shape, you can gradually do more strenuous activity.

Follow a gradual approach to exercise to get the most benefits with the fewest risks. If you have not been exercising, start at a slow pace and, as you become more fit, gradually increase the amount of time and the pace of your activity. Spend about five minutes before each exercise period by stretching all your muscles to give your body a chance to warm up. After you exercise, take another five minutes to cool down with a slower exercise.

It doesn't make sense to kill yourself by exercising too hard in order to have a healthy heart; keep to a comfortable pace (especially at first). For example, you should be able to hold a conversation while you briskly walk or jog. If you feel totally exhausted, feel faint or weak, or have trouble breathing more than ten minutes after your exercise is over, you're exercising too hard.

Choose activities that you enjoy and that fit your personality. For example, if you like team sports or group activities, choose things such as soccer or an aerobics class. If you prefer individual activities, choose things such as swimming or walking. Also, plan your activities for a time of day that suits your personality. If you are a morning person, exercise before you begin the rest of your day's activities. If you have more energy in the evening, plan activities that can be done at the end of the day. You will be more likely to stick to a physical activity program if it is convenient and enjoyable.

MORE IS BETTER

While a little bit of exercise is good, more may be even better. In fact, the National Runners Health Study has found that the farther you run, the better off you are. After studying the running habits of nearly nine thousand men and women, researchers found that all the major risk factors for heart disease dropped as mileage increased. This means that "bad" (LDL) cholesterol and blood pressure readings dropped, "good" (HDL) cholesterol rose, and blood sugar levels improved. Those folks who ran more than 36 miles a week had the best overall blood test scores.

So you will benefit more if you're physically active regularly for longer periods or at greater intensity—but don't overdo it. Remember, too much exercise can give you sore muscles and increase the risk of injury. Stretching and strengthening exercises such as weight training should also be part of your physical activity program. In addition to using calories, these exercises strengthen your muscles and bones and help prevent injury.

EXERCISE REGULARLY

To gain the most health benefits, it's important to make exercise a regular part of your day. If you choose activities that fit into your schedule, it will be easier to keep doing them. Wear shoes that fit and clothes that move with you, and always exercise in a safe location, such as an indoor shopping mall or a school track. Encourage family or friends to join you, and try to get your kids in on the act. If you're active, it's much more likely that your kids will also enjoy exercising and that they'll stay active for the rest of their lives.

SET GOALS

It's a good idea to set both short-term and long-term goals and celebrate every success, no matter how small. Whether your goal is to control your weight or just to feel healthier, becoming physically active is a step in the right direction. Take advantage of the health benefits that regular exercise can offer and make physical activity a part of your lifestyle.

It's a good idea to begin a sensible exercise program gradually. If you've got very high blood pressure, however, it's essential for you to get that under control before you start any type of exercise program. If you start to lift weights with a heart that isn't working efficiently or blood that can't flow easily through wide, smooth arteries, you're just hurrying along the artery injury process

Find Your Target Heart Rate

To get the most health benefits from your aerobic activity, you should exercise at a level strenuous enough to raise your heart rate to your target zone. Your target heart rate zone is 60 percent to 80 percent of the fastest your heart can beat (maximum heart rate). To find your target heart rate zone, first calculate your maximum heart rate by subtracting your age from 220. Multiply this maximum by 60 percent; this is the lower end of your target heart rate zone. Then multiply your maximum heart rate by 80 percent; this is the upper end of your target heart rate zone.

For example, let's say you're fifty years old. To find your target heart rate zone, first find your maximum heart rate by subtracting 50 from 220, giving you 170. Then multiply 170 by 60 percent, which is 102. Then multiply 170 by 80 percent, which is 136. To exercise at training level, you must keep your heart rate between 102 and 136 beats per minute (between 60 and 80 percent of your maximum heart rate).

To see if you are exercising within your target heart rate zone, count the number of pulse beats at your wrist or neck for fifteen seconds, then multiply by 4 to get the beats per minute. Your heart should be beating within your target heart rate zone. If your heart is beating faster than your target heart rate, you are exercising too hard—slow down! If your heart is beating slower than your target heart rate, you need to pick up the pace a little bit. Try to exercise within this target heart rate zone for at least thirty minutes each time you exercise.

When you begin your exercise program, aim for the lower end of your target zone (60 percent). But as you get in better shape, slowly build up to the higher end of your target zone (80 percent). However, if exercising within your target zone seems too hard, then exercise at a pace that is comfortable for you. As you become more comfortable exercising, you'll be able to slowly increase to your target zone.

I described earlier in this book. If you've ever read about a seemingly healthy athlete who dropped dead in the middle of a practice run, this was probably a person who seemed healthy on the outside but whose arteries were a mess on the inside.

A WORD ABOUT WEIGHT LOSS

Losing weight can help reduce inflammation and CRP levels, according to a study published in the April 9, 2003, issue of the *Journal of the American Medical Association*. The study enrolled 120 premenopausal, obese women aged twenty to forty-six who did not have diabetes or high blood pressure. Sixty of the women were randomly selected to receive detailed advice about how to lose weight through exercise and a low-calorie Mediterranean-style diet. The other sixty (the control group) were given general information about healthy food choices and exercise. After two years of follow-up, the women in the first group consumed more complex carbohydrates, more monounsaturated fats, fewer calories, and less cholesterol than the control group. This group also demonstrated a bigger decrease in weight, CRP levels, and insulin resistance. The researchers concluded that such a multidisciplinary program to reduce body weight in obese women through lifestyle changes was associated with a reduction in CRP.

Apple Shape

Obese women, particularly those who carry the bulk of their weight in their abdomens ("apple shape"), are more prone to a type of low-grade inflammation that may increase their risk of heart disease and stroke, according to new study findings. Losing weight, however, can lower their risk. In this study, investigators discovered that so-called apple-shaped women were more likely to have active platelets that lead to more blood clots and higher risk of heart attack and stroke. These women also tended to have a greater degree of free-radical damage (free radicals are by-products of normal metabolism that damage the body's cells, leading to a number of different diseases). Although weight loss is the primary recommendation for obese women, low-dose aspirin may be considered for some women who fail to lose weight, since aspirin can reduce inflammation in the body.

In the study, researchers studied ninety-three obese and twenty-four normal women. Some of the obese women were "apple shaped," carrying most of their weight in their abdomen, while others carried their excess weight on their hips and thighs ("pear shape"). Apple-shaped women are at higher risk of heart disease than their pear-shaped peers. In the study, twenty apple-shaped women followed a 1,200-calorie daily diet for twelve weeks. Both groups of obese women had higher levels of free-radical stress than women who were not obese, but levels among apple-shaped women were markedly higher than levels among pear-shaped women. Levels of CRP were also higher in apple-shaped women, and a twelve-week, low-calorie diet reduced their levels of insulin and CRP.

Heart Disease Risk Reduced

Regular exercise decreases CRP levels as well as the risk of heart disease and may reduce subclinical inflammation, according to two reports; a new study of women from different ethnic backgrounds provides further evidence. This may work because high CRP values are seen in people with infections, while fitness is reported to enhance immune cell activity, leading to resistance to infections.

IN THE NEXT CHAPTER

Eating a good diet and getting plenty of exercise are two great ways to make a start on a healthy heart. But stress can raise CRP levels, too. In the next chapter, we'll discuss ways to de-stress your life.

6

How to De-Stress Your Life

Dan was what I'd call a poster boy for stressful living. As a senior member of a local investment firm, he enjoyed years of unprecedented returns in the stock market: clients made money and so did Dan.

All that changed several years ago when the market underwent a correction; as profits vanished, so did many previously loyal clients. Dan hadn't smoked since college, but with the stress, it wasn't long before he picked up the habit again. As the stress mounted, he gained weight and his blood pressure rose.

None of Dan's friends and colleagues were surprised when they heard he had been admitted to the hospital with chest pain. Fortunately, the amount of heart damage he'd accumulated was small. Dan remembered vividly how the first day in the hospital after surgery was so different from his usual day. Suddenly he had time for reflection—such as how he felt when he missed his daughter's sixteenth birthday. Dan realized how much he'd been neglecting his family by spending so much time at work. Several years later, Dan admitted to me that his anger at missing his daughter's birthday motivated him to change his entire life.

These days, you can find Dan arranging flowers in his brother's florist shop. He sold his BMW, and he and his wife exercise together every day. He tells me he's never been happier. I can just about guarantee his heart is a lot healthier these days, too.

Cardiologists know that for many people, stress, anger, and hostility are a deadly mixture that leads to elevated CRP levels, high blood pressure, and eventually cardiovascular disease. Stress can lead to overeating, smoking, and other behaviors that are detrimental to heart health.

THE BASIC STRESS RESPONSE

When the human body encounters a frightening or stressful situation, it switches into an automatic "fight-or-flight" mode. Your breathing speeds up to prepare you for action. Your heart rate and blood pressure soar as your body produces the stress hormones cortisol and epinephrine (also called adrenaline), boosting heart rate, blood pressure, and metabolism to help you run or fight.

For our ancestors, the fight-or-flight mechanism was important to survival. Today we maintain the same unconscious physical response to stress without the concomitant need to take physical action. When stress hormones are continuously pumped through your body, they can begin to injure your arteries. When the stressful moment is over, the stress hormones should drop to normal. But sometimes they don't; sometimes they stay at high levels in the blood. And when one stress piles on top of another, the stress hormones may never drop below the "crisis" level in your blood.

You probably have no idea how many small, irritating, stressful situations you experience during the day—but odds are, your body knows. Dealing with annoying telemarketers, getting stopped for a speeding ticket, trying to return a sweater without the sales receipt—none of these situations is life threatening, but all create stress. When you're under stress, you may try to control your reactions. But what you end up doing is internalizing them. I'm positive you don't even realize how many tiny, inconsequential, yet annoying stresses you deal with and move on.

If you don't realize that you're monumentally stressed, then you can't do anything about it. If you don't think you've got stress in your life, try what I often recommend to my patients: keep a stress log of just one day of your life.

Keep a Log

Tomorrow morning, as soon as you wake up, grab a pad and jot down each stressful episode, no matter how small. Write down when

- you wake up twenty minutes late because the alarm didn't go off
- your glasses aren't on the nightstand where they should be

- you didn't have time to pick up your best suit from the cleaners and you have nothing else to wear
- there are no clean socks in your drawer
- no one emptied the dishwasher last night and there's no place to put the dirty dishes
- your son suddenly remembers he has a math test today and needs a new protractor
- you're out of the "yellow cheese" your daughter has to have in her lunch, and now she's crying

Before the morning is over, you'll probably already have logged quite a few minor, everyday moments of stress that usually pass you right by. Whether you work inside or outside the home, just trying to get through all the everyday irritations can create a huge burden of stress. Think about it: as each small stress mounts up, your body is pumping out stress hormones that have nowhere to go. Years of these repeated stresses can cripple your immune system, shut down processes that repair your tissues, damage your heart, block sleep, and break down your bones. Such a situation can further lead to anxiety, depression, heart palpitations, and muscle aches.

STRESS AND THE HEART

Stress is particularly hard on the heart. As your body's fight-or-flight response boosts your heart's demand for oxygen, it cuts the body's supply of oxygen at the same time. Meanwhile, stress hormones (adrenaline and cortisol) are pouring into your bloodstream, thickening the blood, and helping to form blood clots that stick to your artery walls or move along into narrower arteries or capillaries, where they can trigger a heart attack or stroke. Studies have found high blood pressure spikes in response to stress are linked to thickened carotid artery walls—and the higher the blood pressure, the thicker the walls.

All kinds of stress can damage the heart. For example, one study found that job stress—especially among people without much control over their daily job responsibilities—can chronically raise blood pressure.

Clinical evidence suggests that emotional stress and anxiety are associated with coronary artery disease and sudden death from heart attacks. Many experts believe that the high levels of stress hormones can contribute to heart disease. Research has shown that heart attacks are most likely to occur in the morning, when both cortisol and blood pressure are at peak levels.

And in one Duke University study, heart patients dramatically reduced their chance of having additional heart problems by using stress reduction techniques such as the ones I'll be discussing shortly. Although many studies have linked emotional stress with an increase risk of heart attacks, the Duke research found that stress reduction can actually reduce the risk.

ARE YOU BREATHING CORRECTLY?

You may not realize it, but most people breathe incorrectly, taking shallow breaths instead of deep, cleansing breaths. Deep breathing is essential for good health and reducing stress; in fact, it's the single most effective way you can ease anxiety.

Poor breathing techniques worsen under stress. Most people take shallow "chest" breaths when they are stressed, so that only the top of their lungs fill with air, depriving the brain of oxygen. This triggers an increase in stress hormones, which further increases their stress. If you sometimes feel a tight band around your chest, feel light-headed, or feel anxious under stress, then you're breathing too shallowly. Here's what happens:

As you start to get anxious in a stressful situation, you start to use your chest muscles to inhale instead of breathing from your diaphragm. Your brain notices the drop in oxygen level and triggers the release of stress chemicals into your blood. This sets up a vicious cycle: the more pronounced the shallow breathing, the more your brain pumps out stress hormones and the more anxious you become. Now you feel even more tense, and if the cycle continues, you may even begin to panic. Your brain gets less oxygen than ever and sends out even more stress hormones.

To fully understand what happens when you breathe from your chest, try this exercise:

1. Lie down and contract your abdominal muscles as hard as you can.
2. Now as you breathe, notice that only your chest rises as you inhale.
3. Pay attention to the way your diaphragm stays in place as the air fills

only the upper portion of your lungs. The way you're breathing as you suck in your stomach is an exaggerated form of the improper way you've been breathing all along.

4. Now, relax your stomach muscles and breathe into your abdomen. See how your diaphragm moves down as the lower portions of your lungs fill up? How do the two different types of breathing make you feel?

Poor breathing habits usually mean that you forget to contract your abdominal muscles and completely exhale so that you're left with stale air in your lower lungs. You need to learn to inhale and exhale correctly to get the most oxygen and remove all the carbon dioxide.

Breathe Deeply

Deep breathing using your diaphragm is a very effective method of relaxation that boosts oxygen exchange, lowers heart rate and blood pressure, distracts you, and increases your sense of control. It includes everything from simple deep breaths to yoga and Zen meditation, and it's an important part of progressive muscle relaxation, relaxation imagery, and meditation. If you can control your breathing, you can control your heart rate and most other stress symptoms. In fact, deep breathing is essential for your health and stress management. Of all the things you can do to ease stress, forming healthy breathing habits is likely to produce the most dramatic results. There is probably no single step that will so profoundly affect your body.

Improve Your Breathing

Let's start with a simple technique to improve your breathing. To increase the amount of oxygen you receive, try this exercise at least once a day for three weeks. It will help you learn the basic approach to switching from shallow to deep breathing, and the more often you do it, the better the results:

1. First, sit up with your back straight.
2. Inhale deeply but gently through your nose.

3. As your breathe, let your abdomen expand. Imagine air filling your abdomen. (This may be challenging, because most of us are so used to *contracting* our abdomen.)
4. Fully expand your chest and lungs with one continuous breath.
5. Slowly breathe out through your nose (this takes longer than inhaling).
6. Breathe this way for at least a minute; keeping your breathing deep and full.

You can use deep breathing whenever you feel tense, and you can even use it to *prevent* some stress symptoms. Try practicing it throughout your day—as you drive to work, prepare for a run before dinner, or get ready to give a speech at work.

Move Your Diaphragm

To breathe correctly, you've got to move your diaphragm, just the way singers do. Here's a way to really understand what I'm talking about:

- Lie down and take a deep, slow breath. Notice any chest movement.
- Put your hand on your abdomen and allow your stomach to rise about an inch as you breathe in.
- As you breathe out, your abdomen will fall about an inch as your chest rises slightly at the same time.
- Notice your diaphragm moving down as you inhale and back up as you exhale. (Remember, you can't correctly breathe from your abdomen if your diaphragm isn't moving down—and your diaphragm can't move down if your stomach muscles are tight.) Relax your stomach muscles.

Deep breathing works by boosting your oxygen exchange and lowering your heart rate and blood pressure. It also distracts you from stressful thoughts and boosts your sense of control. When you know you can count on deep breathing to calm yourself down, you regain a sense of control over your emotions, and the cycle of anxiety is broken.

There are a variety of ways you can practice deep breathing (also called *diaphragmatic breathing*). You can practice in any position, but while you're learning, it's probably best to practice while lying down.

Complete Breathing

This form of deep breathing is very calming and will allow you to breathe in about ten times more air than usual, which will help you increase your lung capacity and clear your air passages. This method uses every part of the lungs.

1. Place your palms at the sides of your ribs with your fingers around to the front, and relax your abdominal muscles.
2. Inhale, expanding your rib cage sideways. As you inhale, try to push your hands apart.
3. Remove your hands and fill your lungs from bottom to top, taking two counts each for the bottom, middle, and top of your lungs.
4. Don't lift your shoulders as you breathe air into the upper part of your lungs.
5. Feel your throat tighten, which lifts the ribs up and out to allow more air into the lungs.
6. Exhale from top to bottom of your lungs, relaxing the throat. As you breathe out, squeeze the ribs from the sides, bringing the fingers of your two hands closer. Contract the rib cage area and then contract the abdominal muscles completely.
7. Now breathe in, and try to push your hands apart.

When to Use Deep Breathing

It's hard for most of us to breathe deeply all the time, but you should try it whenever you feel mildly tense, anxious, or upset. In fact, you can even *prevent* certain stress symptoms (those feelings of stomach butterflies, dry mouth, and pounding heart) by practicing deep breathing before a stressful situation.

You can also use these deep-breathing exercises in the face of severe stress. It's one of the techniques that experts teach patients who are struggling to conquer phobias—the most severe type of stress situation there is.

Deep breathing won't render you unconscious or hypnotize you into doing something you'd regret. It will restore your natural, healthy style of breathing and in the process distract you from pain or anxiety, boost your energy, and sharpen your awareness.

Quick-Fix Breathing

Whenever you're trapped in a stressful situation, here's how you can use breathing to ease that stress. To release your tension and enable yourself to respond calmly:

1. Take several slow, deep breaths.
2. Return to normal breathing.
3. Take several more slow, deep breaths.

If you still feel tense, drop your shoulders and release your stress. Stretching is a great way to do that, and in the next section we'll discuss how it works.

STRETCH AWAY YOUR STRESS

Ideally, you should stretch your muscles every thirty minutes during the day; if you can't, then at least try to stretch early in the morning, at midmorning, at lunch, in midafternoon, and at the end of the day. You've got more than four hundred different skeletal muscles inside your body, and each one of them contracts when it's working and lengthens when it's relaxed. Stretching aids circulation and oxygen flow while reducing muscular tension, and you'll feel energized after you exercise because of the increased flow of oxygen to your body. Moreover, uncomfortable emotions, such as fear, anxiety, resentment, or anger, causes muscles to contract. Stretching relaxes these tense muscles.

Neck Stretch

If you've ever had a tension headache, you know how tight the muscles in the back of your neck can get. Periodically stretching this vulnerable area can help ease tension here. Here's how:

1. Lift your shoulders up to your ears.
2. Rotate your neck and head in large circles three times in each direction.

3. If tilting your head backward hurts, draw imaginary circles with your nose.

Shoulder Shrugs

If you've been sitting in one place all day, either behind the wheel of a car or at a desk at work, the muscles in the middle of your back can really start to protest; this also can lead to tension headaches. To release this tension, try these shoulder shrugs:

1. Rotate your shoulders in a large circle.
2. Push your shoulder blades together, lifting your shoulders as close to your ears as possible.
3. Curl shoulders forward.
4. Pull shoulders toward the floor.
5. Rotate slowly three times in each direction.

Alternatively, try this:

1. Hold your right arm just below the elbow with your left hand.
2. Pull your elbow toward your left shoulder.
3. Hold for three breaths.
4. Repeat on the other side.

If you combine the stretching exercises with deep breathing, you'll be on your way to reducing the amount of stress in your life. You can use the exercises to prevent stress from starting or to ease stress once it happens.

RELAXATION: THE FIRST STEPS

Now that you've learned the correct way to breathe and how to stretch your muscles, it's time to learn a bit more about how to do relaxation exercises and meditate. When you relax, either from whole-body relaxation exercises, meditation, or visualization, your breathing slows, your blood pressure drops, your muscles relax, anxiety lessens, stressful thoughts and headaches disappear, irritability eases, and focus and concentration improve.

When to Relax

Many people find it helpful to schedule a relaxation or meditation moment each day. "Morning people" like to start off the day with a meditation or relaxation period of twenty minutes or so; others prefer to use these techniques to unwind after a hard day. Still others (especially those with extremely stress-filled jobs) find they perform best when using part of their lunch hour to relax or meditate.

How to Relax Your Muscles

The first thing to learn is how to relax your body, which isn't so easy if you're feeling stressed. It's important to remember not to go about trying to relax with as much gusto as you do everything else. You don't have to worry about doing it "right," doing it "enough," or whether it's taking too long. Relaxing is really a process of letting go.

As you begin, you'll probably be surprised at how much tension you find in your muscles. Until you learn to consciously relax your muscles, you may not realize how rigid and tight some of those muscles are. Here's the simple way to relax each muscle group:

1. Find a position that feels comfortable, either sitting or lying down.
2. Close your eyes.
3. Relax your arms with hands slightly folded on your lap or at your sides if you are lying down.
4. Begin taking slow, deep breaths.
5. Breath rhythmically from the abdomen, not the chest.
6. Say the word "relax" silently to yourself as you consciously relax the muscles at the top of your head.
7. When you feel the top of your head relax, move down to your face. Keep repeating "relax" as you consciously focus on each muscle group in your face. Don't move on until you can feel that area relax. Move on to the sinus area of your face, and whisper "relax."

8. Spend more time on the muscles at the back of your neck, where a lot of your stress is probably concentrated. Don't continue until you can actually feel those muscles loosen.
9. Move down all the way to your toes, relaxing each section of your body.

Progressive Muscle Relaxation (PMR)

There are many different relaxation methods. If you don't think you can ease your muscles by simply focusing on a muscle and willing it to relax, try this:

1. Close your eyes and sit or lie down comfortably.
2. Relax your arms with hands slightly folded on your lap or at your sides.
3. Begin taking slow, deep breaths.
4. Breath rhythmically from your abdomen (check that your stomach pushes out).
5. Beginning with the muscles at the back of your head, firmly tighten just those muscles. Hold for five seconds, and then relax them. It's important to keep the rest of your body relaxed while you're tensing one group of muscles. (This isn't as easy as it sounds!)
6. As you relax each muscle, focus on how the muscle feels and visualize the muscle becoming relaxed.
7. If you have trouble tensing and relaxing different groups of muscles, practice first with your fist. Clench it tightly, and then relax. This is what you should be aiming for with each muscle group.
8. As you relax the muscle, imagine white light and warm energy filling the area. (If you have trouble visualizing white light, imagine a thick mist or fog.)
9. Work your way down your body, tensing and relaxing one muscle group at a time. Concentrate on keeping the rest of your body relaxed.

Countdown Relaxation

Here's another good method to practice total-body relaxation:

1. First do a progressive relaxation of all muscles.

2. Count down slowly from ten to one, and visualize the numbers in front of you.
3. At the same time, imagine you are riding down an escalator or floating downward on a cloud.
4. When you get to the bottom, imagine you are in a lovely relaxing place.

MEDITATION

Now that you've learned how to enter a state of light relaxation, you can experiment with a deeper relaxed state—meditation. It's clear that a deep state of meditation provides benefits for your entire body, including your cardiovascular system. Here's how:

1. Follow the steps in Countdown Relaxation to relax your body.
2. As you breathe out, empty your mind, and silently repeat a word or a phrase (such as "peace").
3. You may be surprised at how hard it is to empty your mind. When thoughts pop into your head—and they will—let them go calmly. Return to your word.
4. Practice for ten or fifteen minutes at first; you may want to extend your meditation as you become more experienced.

After several weeks of practice, most people feel not just more relaxed after meditating, but more likely to stay calm in response to stress. However, meditation doesn't work for everyone. Some people say they get so relaxed they simply drift off to sleep. And others become more stressed because they can't master the art of thinking about nothing. If this is your problem, you might have more success at visualizing—a form of relaxation in which instead of emptying your mind, you give your mind something to think about.

VISUALIZATION

Visualization is a more active procedure than meditation, and many high-stressed people who have trouble sitting still find that visualizing is easier than meditating because they are actually *doing* something with their mind. Basically, when you practice visualization, you're first relaxing your body and then vividly imagining yourself in a peaceful scene. The principle behind successful visualization and imagery is that by using your mind to re-create a relaxing place and then by placing yourself in that scene, you will actually feel more relaxed. The more vividly you call up the scene in your mind, the stronger and more realistic the experience will be. Some people find it very relaxing simply to imagine themselves lolling by a sun-splashed beach, hearing the waves crash on the sand or wild birds singing in a meadow.

Vividly imagining can be almost as effective as reality. Your sense organs convert signals from your environment into nerve impulses that feed into parts of your brain that interpret the environment. When you practice visualization, you're creating a similar set of nerve impulses. Because your brain can't tell the difference between what is real and what is actively imagined, this type of active visualization can truly make a difference in the way you deal with everyday situations. It's a trick that professional athletes have used for years to improve their performance. You can do the same thing.

Some people aren't content to simply visualize a relaxing scene; they prefer the challenge of actually *doing something* while in this relaxing place. This is called *active visualization*, and it starts the same way. But after you have imagined yourself in a peaceful place, you can then give yourself positive suggestions while you're in the scene. These are called *affirmations,* and they work much like a hypnotic suggestion. Here's how it works:

1. First, perform a total-body relaxation as described earlier.
2. When you are completely relaxed, imagine a calm, beautiful scene in full detail, keeping your eyes closed. You can choose a place you've visited in the past or create your own magical arena. (This may take practice; some people are gifted visualizers, but more concrete thinkers may find this challenging.)
3. Remember, the more vivid, the better. *Hear* the trees move in the breeze. *Smell* the salty air of the ocean. *Feel* the sun gently warming your face.
4. As you remain at the scene with your eyes closed, give yourself a positive affirmation: "My breathing is gentle and calm." "I feel completely relaxed in every social situation." "My blood is flowing gently through wide, healthy arteries."

5. Keep the affirmations *positive*. Don't say, "I've got to lose ten pounds." Say, "I feel light as a feather and totally in shape" or "I enjoy eating fresh vegetables and healthy fruits." Don't say, "I've got to stop feeling so tense!" Instead, suggest, "I will feel calm in every situation."

6. At the end of the visualization, tell yourself, "When I open my eyes, I will feel peaceful and completely refreshed." Then open your eyes, and prepare to be amazed!

Visualize Anytime!

Visualizations can help you de-stress after a busy day at work. To prepare yourself when you know you're heading into a stressful situation, "preview" the upcoming situation, imagining yourself acting confidently and calmly. The more chances you have to preview a situation, the more likely you'll be able to get through it just the way you've imagined it.

For Stubborn Cases

If you're having a really hard time with stress, try these tips:

- When you imagine yourself in the middle of a relaxing scene, picture stress actually flowing out of your body. If you have trouble visualizing this, liken the stress to water. Now try again.
- If you can't seem to control your stress, visualize a huge wooden trunk; picture yourself folding your worries or stress away and locking it away in the trunk.
- Those of you who are prone to worry as you lie in bed tossing and turning can try this one: As soon as you start to concentrate on a stressful concern, visualize a large wastebasket right by your bed. Visualize yourself taking each worry, one by one, and throwing it away. If you like, you can tell yourself that tomorrow you'll fish them out and worry then.
- Don't be surprised if you find yourself resisting some of these suggestions. Often, obsessive worrying has become such a habit that

we are actually more comfortable worrying than *not* worrying. Your mind may balk at giving up stressful thoughts—but if you persevere, you'll succeed.

ALTERNATE STRESS BUSTERS

If you feel uncomfortable doing relaxation exercises, meditating, or visualizing, you may be glad to know that any quiet pursuit (such as reading or spending time on a hobby) is also moderately effective in helping you relax. To reach a deeper state of relaxation—which is most helpful in reducing stress—try one of the following alternatives.

Listen to Music

Scientists have found that listening to music can reduce stress, slow your heart rate, and lower your blood pressure. To get the most benefit, it's probably better to choose soothing classical music over harsh or loud tunes; slow music is more soothing than fast, strings and woodwinds are more soothing than trumpets or discordant electric sounds, and instrumentals are better than trying to follow the words to a song.

When you're feeling especially stressed, start out with music that matches your angry or agitated mood. Then gradually change the music to reflect the mood you want to attain: something soothing and calming with a smooth, relaxing flow. Or try a selection of "environmental" music—summer rain, woods noises, wind and surf with seagulls.

Steam Away Your Stress

Many people insist a hot shower, bath, sauna, or hot tub steams away their stress by easing tightened muscles and lowering blood pressure. If you arrive home with a tension headache, you can often find relief by standing under a hot shower. Some experts believe the hot steamy water also triggers the release of brain chemicals that produce a sense of well-being while lowering the level of stress hormones. Finally, a hot bath before bed appears to result in deeper, more restful sleep—another good way to ward off stress. For an added benefit, add fragrant herbs, such as lavender or sandalwood, to the bathwater.

Pet Your Pet

Scientists have found that there's a real health benefit in petting a dog or cat. Stroking an animal actually reduces blood pressure and eases stress—in both the human *and* the pet. Even the presence of a dog or a tankful of fish in a room seems to help people relax. Of course, for some people, owning a dog or cat in the first place could create its own stress, so choose your pet wisely.

Have a Good Laugh

A good belly laugh can work wonders on your heart rate, blood pressure, and CRP levels and diffuse stressful situations. Scientists have found that the process is similar to what happens during aerobic exercise. When you laugh, your blood pressure, heart rate, and muscle tension rise briefly. Then your blood pressure drops, and you become more relaxed. This is why you'll find many hospitals and nursing homes providing humor magazines, comics, or humorous videos and tapes for their patients.

You can do the same. Stock up on humorous tapes, videos, and books. Then reach for one of these when you're feeling totally stressed out.

Get a Massage

A therapeutic massage is guaranteed to ease your stress if you have time to take one. Massage can dramatically reverse the damaging physiological effects of stress by helping to lower heart rate and blood pressure, boost circulation, warm the skin, make you feel better, and reduce anxiety. During the massage, your tight muscles relax, and the pain that comes with chronic tension dissolves. As your circulation gets a boost, your muscles receive more oxygen and nutrients.

Exercise Regularly

It may seem odd, but exercising—by releasing tension that's built up in your body—can be surprisingly relaxing. And it's been proven to lower CRP levels and improve heart health.

Consider a Therapist

When stress builds up, it can affect the way you think about your job, your personality, your family, and ultimately your health. If the methods we've discussed in this chapter don't seem to help, you may want to consult a mental health professional to help you handle your stress and fears and help you plan for the future. If you can't afford mental health care, your minister, priest, or rabbi may provide counseling at no cost to you. Here are some signs that your stress has reached crisis levels and you need professional help:

- you feel depressed most of the time
- you have violent or angry feelings a lot
- you've been drinking more than usual
- you get mean when you drink
- you feel you can't cope

IN THE NEXT CHAPTER

Now that you've learned how to breathe and relax away your stress, it's time to learn how to make some vital lifestyle changes in the way you approach life psychologically. Keep in mind that your mind and your body are intimately connected, so that how you feel about yourself and your life directly affects the health of your entire cardiovascular system.

7

Lifestyle Changes

Your living is determined not so much by what life brings to you as by the attitude you bring life; not so much by what happens to you as by the way your mind looks at what happens.

JOHN HOMER MILLER

Brian and Jeff were both smokers in their forties who were admitted to my hospital with heart attacks. They both received intravenous medication to dissolve the blood clots responsible for their heart attacks, and both men underwent balloon angioplasty to treat their blockages. Yet despite these similarities, they responded to their illness in very different ways.

Both men were educated about risk factors, prevention, and smoking cessation, and they attended cardiac rehabilitation together. Brian completed the full ten-week session, but Jeff dropped out after four weeks. Three months after their discharge from the hospital, Jeff was still smoking, whereas Brian had not only quit, but had also lost 12 pounds!

The differences in how these two men responded to their heart attacks intrigued me, so I spent a lot of time asking them questions in an effort to understand why they had such different attitudes.

Jeff was a car salesman who spent long hours at the dealership, which took a toll on his marriage. He had two children from his first wife, one with his second wife, and he'd been separated four months when he had his heart attack. He readily appreciated the fact he was under considerable stress at the dealership, what with the constant pressure to sell more cars than in the previous quarter. He felt he didn't have enough time to exercise. When I asked him what he did for fun, he thought for a long time. Finally, he simply shook his head no as a tear slid down his cheek. It was clear Jeff was suffering from clinical depression, a very real medical illness associated with abnormal chemical levels in the brain. Clinical depression is fairly common after a heart attack.

At the time of his heart attack, Brian had been married to his wife Carol for eighteen years and had two children. A day before Brian's discharge, I asked him whether he thought he would return to smoking. He told me he refused to "lie down and let the damn tobacco companies declare victory over yet another soul." Over those first several months, Brian shared with me his secret for suppressing the urge to light up; he simply envisioned his children, then ages eight and twelve, growing up without a dad. Unlike Jeff, Brian had a loving family and a strong personal support system.

We physicians need to do a better job of listening to our patients. Research tells us that the average doctor interrupts a patient within the first eleven seconds. This is really a shame, because over the years my patients have taught me a lot. By careful listening, I've learned the tools that successful patients use to enhance their survival.

It is important to remember that there are no cures for heart blockage; an artery that gets blocked once will probably block up again or get worse. If changes are not made after the initial diagnosis, the blockage will likely progress. Patients need to attack heart disease in many different ways to keep it from progressing.

Much power lies in the patient's hands. People *choose* to smoke or not smoke. People *choose* to eat sensibly or poorly. People *choose* to exercise or not. People *choose* to deal with stress in healthy or unhealthy ways. These are choices we make every day.

Jeff's choices were quite destructive and influenced heavily by depression; Brian chose to start living a healthy lifestyle. These choices made a profound difference in their outcomes. What makes one patient look at problems and attack them ferociously to overcome the odds, while another makes only a half-hearted effort and ultimately fails? Can the healthy approach be identified? Might it be useful to others as an addition to standard treatments? Might this approach offer help to those struggling with other diseases? My patients have taught me the answer to all these questions is *yes*!

The tools to change your lifestyle come from my observations of patients over the years. I've seen patients who have lived full, happy lives despite severe congestive heart failure or other heart problems. Those patients who succeed have four characteristics:

1. A healthy sense of perspective
2. A sense of wonder
3. A sense of humor
4. A sense of purpose

The good news is that these characteristics are not inborn—they can be taught. They are an underutilized tool that can help you improve your own health. Unlike medicines and surgical procedures, they're free and have no side effects.

A HEALTHY SENSE OF PERSPECTIVE

Carl suffered his first heart attack when he was thirty-four; he spent six weeks in an oxygen tent. Fifteen years later, he suffered another heart attack. Still later, he developed colon and prostate cancer. And he lived the last eight years of his life with chronic lymphocytic leukemia.

You'd never guess his formal education ended with high school, because Carl was one of the most intelligent, engaging individuals I ever met. He was surrounded by a calm peace, and the office staff were always happy to see him. When I asked him how he has dealt with all his medical problems, he quoted Milton: "The mind is its own place, and in itself can make a heaven of hell, a hell of heaven."

Carl and patients like him have taught me the power of perspective. Plane crashes and lottery winnings are rare events; most things in life are various shades of gray. How we "spin" these events in our mind colors the fabric of our daily life. It's not surprising that a negative outlook often leads to unhealthy behaviors; we find temporary solace in a trip to the refrigerator or the corner store for cigarettes. We're less inclined to exercise or take our medication.

Patients who have a healthy sense of perspective realize they have a choice in how they view life events. We each make these choices every day of our lives. How much does it really matter that you locked your keys in the car? Does it really matter that you didn't get the promotion you thought you deserved? Should you allow these events to overshadow other aspects of your life?

Another patient taught me the "one hundred year rule": Since one hundred years from now you and everyone you know will be dead, is this particular problem worth worrying about? Life events cannot command your negative attention unless you let them. It's up to you. You have that much power.

Of course, with power comes responsibility. It is your responsibility to take care of yourself. You have an obligation to eat properly, exercise, take your medication as directed, and avoid nicotine. Most of us aren't dealt four aces and a king in life, so we need to play the hand we're dealt as intelligently as we can.

The first thing to let go of is worry. When I ask my oldest patients (all over ninety years of age) if they have worried during their life, they usually say yes. When I ask if it helps, they invariably laugh and say no. I figure if worrying hasn't helped the most experienced people on the planet, it's not going to help me or the rest of my patients either.

Of course, worrying is part of human nature. If you choose to worry, try using a "worry tree." Pick a tree close to your front door. As the sun sets, go to that tree and take the necklace of problems you have forged throughout your day and place it on the worry tree. Leave all your worries on that tree. Go inside and be with your family or your pet. (If you live alone and don't have a pet, go get one!) The next morning, if you really want to, go to that tree and remove the necklace and put it back around your neck.

A healthy sense of perspective involves the understanding that life events don't always proceed in the way we think they are going to. Life throws curveballs at us all the time. If we change our expectations and learn to expect curveballs, we feel less frazzled when they do come our way.

Life's finite nature and fragility are reinforced daily in the life of a cardiologist. It is much subtler in other walks of life. Cancer patients sometimes say that it may be worth putting up with cancer because of what their cancer has taught them about living their life. Author Bernie Siegel suggests we live our lives as though we had a year to live. We wouldn't ignore our responsibilities, but we would give appropriate priority to those aspects of our lives that mean the most to us. Siegel implores us not to wait to get cancer to learn how to live.

A healthy perspective helps us realize the best things in life aren't things. They are the people (and pets!) we care about and the times we live deeply and fully. Full involvement doesn't mean a hectic schedule. Living fully can be achieved purely and simply. The early-morning walk before the sun rises as we hear each bird greet the new day, can be a downright spiritual experience. And sharing these simple moments with the ones that mean the most to us rewards the heart richly.

A SENSE OF WONDER

Apollo 8 was NASA's penultimate flight prior to attempting a lunar landing. This would also be humankind's first experience in lunar orbit. Human eyes would gaze upon the far side of the moon for the first time.

After liftoff on December 21, 1968, several Earth orbits (to be sure all systems were 'go') concluded with translunar injection, a precisely timed firing of the main rockets to break free of Earth's gravitational field and head to the moon. The tension rose at Mission Control as *Apollo 8* drew closer to its target. The main rocket would need to fire again to slow the spacecraft and allow it to settle into orbit around the moon. There was always the chance something had happened to the rocket during the three-day journey to our nearest celestial neighbor. An improper burn could send the crew into the dark blackness of deep space.

Astronauts Frank Borman, James Lovell, and William Anders slipped behind the moon, out of radio contact with Earth. Flight engineers on the ground in Houston would not know if all went well until the ship emerged from the moon's shadow and line-of-sight radio communications could resume. Houston knew the precise time when Apollo would resume radio contact. Alarmingly, the radio was silent. Ground controllers feared the worst.

The crew of *Apollo 8* were fine. Their engine had burned on time for the exact length of time necessary to achieve lunar orbit. They were about to "call home" as they emerged from the back side of the moon but they were awestruck by a sight no man had ever witnessed before: Earthrise. The gray, lifeless, crater-savaged, back side of the moon gave way to a bright, blue-green jewel suspended in the velvet blackness.

As the crew orbited around the moon, in a live broadcast to earth, they read the opening verses of the book of Genesis. That evening was Christmas Eve.

To say 1968 was a tumultuous year is an understatement. Martin Luther King and Robert Kennedy were murdered. Cities burned that terrible summer with racial tension. North Korea captured the *Pueblo*. The carnage of Vietnam was brought to American television on a nightly basis.

The flight of *Apollo 8* was a gift to the entire world. I can still remember news footage of people around the globe huddled around television sets, watching the progress of *Apollo 8*. For a moment, we were all one people. We lived in the same place—Earth—our home. Our astronauts saw the planet as it was; there were no lines between countries indicating division. Perhaps the vast majority of our problems were indeed, of our own design.

Apollo 8 flew in my thirteenth year. The day after I heard the crew read from Genesis was Christmas. A large present with my name on it commanded my interest. It was from my brother, who was serving his country in Vietnam. I couldn't believe it. A telescope. I don't know if I ever enjoyed a gift more. The optics weren't great and the mount was unsteady, but I didn't know anything different. I spent Christmas night gazing at the moon and whatever else I could find. I observed sunspots the next day with eye protection filters. Such began a lifelong fascination with astronomy.

Spending time looking up at the stars is incredibly therapeutic. There is a fuzzy spot in the northeastern sky in the spring of each year. With good binoculars or a small telescope, the spiral nature of this galaxy is apparent. This jewel is 2.1 million light-years away from us. A light-year is a measure of distance. It is the distance light travels in one year. This light, which strikes my eye, began its journey 2.1 million years ago!

If you notice several stars that don't twinkle, take a look at them with a pair of binoculars. They aren't stars at all, but are planets: Jupiter, Saturn, and Mars are visible to the naked eye much of the year. Jupiter is an especially good look through binoculars because you can see tiny points of light very close to the planet. These are Jupiter's major moons.

Several hundred years ago, Galileo gazed upon the same sight and had an epiphany. He realized this was proof that smaller bodies revolved around larger bodies. It was also proof that Earth was not the center of the universe. We revolved around the sun, obeying the laws of the universe, as did the other planets. Humankind didn't seem to have any particularly noble position in the order of things. With this observation, the Dark Ages were over; an idea corroborated by measured data was the beginning of the scientific method. The world would never be the same again.

I gaze upward for peace and comfort. The shear scale of the universe, the pictures of Earth taken from the moon, and the idea that dinosaurs roamed

Earth when light from distant galaxies began its journey all provide me with perspective. My problems seem quite small in comparison.

A SENSE OF HUMOR

Where would we be if we couldn't laugh at the occasional absurdities in life? American author, orator, and minister Henry Ward Beecher knew that "mirth is God's medicine." My parents have shown me the value of humor. Now in their mid-eighties, they have both had their share of medical problems, which have grown more frequent and serious over time. But despite these problems, they both have a vibrant sense of humor.

They frequently remind me (and anyone else who will listen) of a story from my childhood. We had driven past a tragic automobile accident, where it was clear there were serious injuries. A child of seven years, I asked my parents how Howard would let such a thing happen.

"Howard? Who's Howard?" my father queried.
"God."
"God? You think God's name is Howard?"
"Of course it's Howard," I replied. I can still recall their quizzical expressions.
"Why do you think God's name is Howard?"
"Don't you guys know anything? They tell us in church every time we go: our Father who art in heaven, Howard be thy name!"

Older patients seem to have greater license to tell some stories, which might be looked on differently if a younger person told the same story. Just such a story was told by an eighty-six-year-old man hospitalized in the intensive care unit with advanced congestive heart failure. I was a resident in internal medicine at the time. The attending physician and I greeted this gentleman, who began to ramble on with a story about his pet schnauzer. The attending physician was interested in the story because he also had a schnauzer. The patient explained that his dog took second place in the Westminster Kennel Club show that year, a very prestigious event that piqued the interest of my mentor. The elderly man explained that the reason for missing first place involved the length of the dog's snout hairs. He also explained that one cannot simply trim the hairs with scissors or clippers; rather, the ends must be touched with depilatory cream. The attending physician listened intently.

"In fact, my daughter was at the pharmacy just yesterday to pick up some Nair," the patient continued. "The pharmacist cautioned her not to put on her blouse for a half hour after using the product. She told him it wasn't for her underarms but for her schnauzer. He then said: 'Well, in that case, don't ride a bike for a week'!"

It took a moment for us both to realize we had been hooked and played like a trout by this wily character. Out of respect for the elderly man, we had listened to what at first had seemed like a mundane story; he had had us in his sights the entire time. The story spread through the hospital. The director of the cafeteria especially enjoyed it; he made sure the patient had whatever he wanted to eat, personally delivered, hot and fresh. For the remaining two years of his life, virtually everyone in the small hospital knew the Schnauzer Man. He was always cared for with extra warmth, and he brightened many an individual's day with the humor he shared.

Humor can also be a wonderful defense mechanism. Our polling place is located near a large retirement community. The last election found me dutifully in line with many older individuals. Even though it was late in the day, the long line wound around the large room. Having just completed hospital rounds, I was still on call for problems or new admissions. I was set with my pager and mobile phone. The room was uncomfortably warm. Perhaps it was my imagination, but many of the room's inhabitants wouldn't stop looking at me. I reasoned it had to do with the height and age difference. I stand six feet six inches, and everyone in line to vote seemed to be four feet eleven inches; I was feeling a little like a lighthouse when I started to grow concerned that if I had to return a call to the hospital, it might reveal my profession to the already interested crowd.

The worst case scenario occurred. I needed to return a call to the hospital. The signal strength indicator on the cell phone gave me a sick feeling as it registered only one of four signal strength bars. I needed to repeatedly shout into the phone that it was Dr. Deron returning a page. While taking the call, I noticed the crowd pressing closer.

No sooner did I complete my call than an older woman closed in. She sought my opinion regarding the foot pain that five doctors over thirty years had not been able to diagnose. People beyond the lady with the foot pain began to press closer. I was convinced they were all mentally composing their medical problem list for my immediate attention. The foot pain lady moved on now to her stomach pain. The crowd pressed closer from all sides. There was no escape.

It was then my survival instincts kicked in and I came up with a devilish idea . . . a little white lie. "Ma'am, I'm sorry I can't help you with your foot problem. You see, I'm a specialist."

"A specialist, oh my!" The crowd pressed in closer to hear the answer to the obvious next question: "What do you specialize in?"

In a loud and clear voice, I responded, "Sexually transmitted diseases." With that the crowd immediately pulled away. I could breathe again. I sped home to share the story with my wife, and we laughed ourselves to sleep that night. Life is too short for us to be too serious.

A SENSE OF PURPOSE

Through the millennia, humans have pondered the fundamental question of why we are here. Is it simple existence from birth to the grave? Is there a greater purpose outside the needs of self? It is this question that may start an individual on a remarkable journey of discovery.

A purposeful existence is a soulful existence—not in any specific theological context, but as human experience that is separate from mind and heart. It is a core trait, the lowest common denominator of thought and being. It is that part of us that speaks to us when we are too tired to hear our mind or our heart.

Care and feeding of the soul is not taught in most secular schools; it doesn't seem to be valued in this society as much as a person's wealth and productivity. There are no bonus points for time spent in the care of the soul. But just as a beautiful garden can't grow without labor, so does a peaceful soul require its own cultivation.

A sense of purpose (and a sense of soul) requires vision beyond what we need to exist. This is a distinctly human characteristic. The awareness and commitment to a purpose beyond ourselves is not found elsewhere in the animal kingdom. There is no greater act than the selfless, unconditional giving of one's self. The reward associated with it is always monumental.

We cannot control the love that others show us, but we can control the love that we extend to others. A life lived in a loving manner is always richly rewarded, for the act of loving becomes its own reward. We free ourselves from the bondage of "What's in it for me?" We are liberated and find peace in the concept "What can I do for others?"

As an assistant scoutmaster in my son's Boy Scout troop, we teach the boys to leave the campsite better than they found it. What a simple, wonderful idea! Imagine if each successive human generation lived in a similar fashion through a loving and caring life; the social and environmental impact would be dramatic.

The satisfaction and contentment attained by living a life with purpose has remarkable health benefits. Brenda is a forty-seven year old who had her first heart attack at the age of thirty-two. She had her first coronary bypass operation two years later. Within four more years, she had her second bypass operation. Despite the usual warnings about smoking, she continued to smoke. She remained dramatically overweight and was never vigilant with her diabetes management.

One bright spring morning, I ran into Brenda at the grocery store, and I was immediately alarmed by her appearance. She had lost 45 pounds and stopped smoking. I was convinced there was an underlying malignancy. I asked her to see me in the office the following week. She was reluctant to do any additional tests because as she explained, she had made all these changes herself.

Brenda explained that she had started volunteering at the local homeless shelter. The fulfillment she experienced from that act enabled her to stop smoking. She was empowered by the people she helped not only to quit smoking but to lose weight as well. She no longer felt the need for the gratification associated with food and tobacco. Over the years it became clear that there wasn't any underlying cancer; it was just change—for the better.

Learning from Brenda's experience, I have recommended that other patients look for volunteer opportunities. It is now clear to me that Brenda's experience was not unique. There is a reproducible benefit realized when we give, and the magnitude of that benefit is often remarkably out of proportion to the benefactor's gift. Brenda read stories to children at the shelter and helped with food preparation. In return, she no longer needs to take insulin, her blood pressure is controlled, and she has remained an ex-smoker for the past eight years. Modern medicine had tried for years in vain to achieve these goals. Brenda's life and health were transformed not by pills and browbeating, but by her simple, unconditional act of love.

Seemingly, many walk around looking for something they never seem to find. They hope it can be found in a new job, car, or relationship. When the new object fails to fill the void, health suffers. Compliance with proper diet and exercise declines. Trips to the refrigerator or corner store for a pack of cigarettes increase. Weight rises. The workload on the heart increases. The door is open to progression of heart disease.

My patients have taught me that working on establishing a benevolent, compassionate lifestyle provides the ultimate satisfaction. The upshot of such an endeavor is that deleterious acts are replaced by benevolent acts. A benevolent act doesn't need to be monumental—it may be a gift of time, or expertise, or perhaps something as simple as a smile.

The life we lead is our choice. We can choose to ask, "What's in it for me?" or "What can I do to make things better?" It has been my observation that those who focus on the former question lead a life without fulfillment. They hope something new will fill the void, but the soul is never nourished. Those who open their hearts with love and compassionate understanding for others find peace through purpose. They are happy in a deep place that is never reached when happiness is sought through external things. And when the individual has found peace through nourishing the soul, the body benefits: blood pressure falls, food is no longer sought as an answer, weight falls, cholesterol and CRP levels fall, and the strain on the heart decreases.

Living for the greater good beyond the individual is the key to purposeful human existence. It is available to anyone. Look at what you have to offer. Whether you read to children, help at your place of worship, pick up trash, or volunteer at a hospital, find some way to make a difference. The rewards are priceless.

IN THE NEXT CHAPTER

Now that you've learned about the four characteristics that can help you live a healthier, richer life, it's time to think about some other things you can control in your fight for a healthier heart. In the next chapter, you'll learn about what effect pills and medications have on your CRP level and your overall health.

8

Pills and Medications

Tom was a forty-five-year old sportswriter with a family history of heart disease and a bad case of asthma, whose blood pressure was spiraling out of control. He often found himself grabbing high-fat lunches and dinners washed down by a few beers at the restaurant around the corner from the newspaper where he worked, and he rarely had time for exercise. When he was unable to control his blood pressure by eating a better diet, eliminating salt, and getting exercise and more sleep, he turned to medication to help control the problem.

If you're at high risk for heart disease, high blood pressure, or stroke, there are plenty of lifestyle changes you should make right away—namely, improve your diet, get more exercise, and stop smoking. To me, these changes are far more desirable than turning to medication, which doesn't always work and which carries the risk of adverse effects. And experts suggest you can cut your heart disease risks by up to 80 percent by making these profound changes in your everyday life.

But if lifestyle strategies just don't work, you may need to consult with your doctor to see if medication might help get your cardiovascular system under control. Today we know that many of these medications work not only by lowering cholesterol or blood pressure, but also by lowering levels of CRP and inflammation.

If you have a higher-than-normal CRP level, your doctor will probably give you three to six months to try to make the appropriate lifestyle changes. If, after all your effort, your CRP is still too high, many doctors will probably decide it's time to add a drug to help control the problelm.

In this situation, I'd start with something fairly mild, such as aspirin; if that doesn't work, it could be time to move more aggressively, toward statins or ACE inhibitors because of their anti-inflammatory action.

ASPIRIN THERAPY

If you've stopped smoking, lost weight, and started eating a healthier diet and your inflammation level is still too high, you might want to ask your doctor if you should take low-dose aspirin. Today, 27 million Americans are taking a daily low-dose tablet to boost their heart health or lower the risk of a second heart attack or stroke.

Aspirin reduces clotting ability and inflammation and has been proven to help treat acute heart attack patients (chewing on an aspirin at the first symptom of a heart attack can cut the risk of death by 25 percent). It also lowers the chance that your arteries will become clogged again after bypass surgery. It works by stopping platelets from adhering to injured artery linings and keeping them from sticking together to form clots. By taking an aspirin a day, you're effectively stopping the formation of plaques in your arteries.

The American Heart Association now recommends that you talk to your doctor about low-strength aspirin to avoid a first heart attack or stroke if you're at high risk of cardiovascular disease. The AHA believes that the benefits of aspirin therapy in lowering the risk of cardiovascular disease outweigh the risk of gastrointestinal side effects in people with a 10 percent risk of heart disease over the next ten years.

Who Should Take Aspirin

A daily aspirin tablet is a good idea for almost everyone. Even if you don't need it, odds are it won't hurt you. Many doctors believe that a daily aspirin tablet is a good idea for men over age forty-five with risk factors, all men over age fifty, and postmenopausal women. This relatively harmless preventive measure costs very little, and it's much cheaper than bypass surgery.

Who Should Not Take Aspirin

While a daily aspirin dose is safe for almost everyone, there are a few people who should not take aspirin because (in rare cases) it might cause other health problems or allergic reactions.

When to Take Aspirin

Ask your doctor about taking a daily aspirin tablet if you have experienced:

- a heart attack
- a stroke
- chest pain (angina)
- a transient ischemic attack (TIA)
- bypass surgery
- balloon angioplasty

When Not to Take Aspirin

Do not take aspirin if you:

- have bleeding in the stomach
- are taking blood thinners, unless your physician approves
- drink a great deal of alcohol
- are allergic to aspirin
- have severe kidney or liver disease
- have an ulcer
- have a history of asthma and nasal polyps (triad asthma)
- have uncontrolled high blood pressure
- have a bleeding disorder
- are pregnant and haven't asked your doctor about aspirin

How Much Aspirin to Take

Most research has recommended a daily dose of between 75 and 150 milligrams of aspirin; today you can buy special "heart healthy" forms of aspirin in 81-milligram doses. (A standard tablet is between 300 and 325 milligrams). While a little is good, you should not assume that more is better, because large doses of aspirin can be harmful. Of course, you should consult with your doctor before taking any medication like this on a regular basis.

Doctors recommend that someone taking aspirin during a suspected heart attack use a standard 325-milligram tablet (or half a tablet) dissolved in water.

No Substitutions

Because of its mild antiplatelet properties, aspirin is the only nonsteroidal anti-inflammatory drug that can be helpful to the cardiovascular system. Although it may seem as if other anti-inflammatory drugs (such as ibuprofen) should also work, research has not yet proven that they are as effective as aspirin. In fact, ibuprofen has been shown to block the beneficial antiplatelet effects of aspirin and ideally should be avoided. (And remember never to take aspirin and ibuprofen at the same time; they will interfere with each other.)

Acetaminophen (Tylenol) should not be substituted for aspirin because it has never been found to have any heart benefits; it does not reduce inflammation, and it doesn't work the same way that aspirin does. Moreover, long-term use of acetaminophen may be harmful to your kidneys.

VITAMINS

If aspirin doesn't work or you can't take it because of a pre-existing condition, you might want to try vitamins. Although vitamin therapy for cardiovascular problems is still a bit controversial, some small studies have suggested that vitamins E, B_6, and C—or a daily multivitamin—are all linked to lower levels of CRP. In at least one small study of seventy-five patients, vitamin E was able to lower CRP levels by about 30 percent after three months of treatment with 1,200 international units (IU).

This should not be surprising, since another recent small study published in the British journal *The Lancet* showed that supplementation with vitamins C and E slows the progression of artery disease in heart transplant patients. Typically, hardening of the arteries develops within three years in 70 percent of these patients.

But when vitamins C (500 milligrams) and E (400 IU) were given twice daily for a year to forty patients who had heart transplants within the last two years, artery thickness barely changed. However, patients who had not taken vitamins experienced an 8 percent increase in coronary artery thickening. Previously, it had been shown that antioxidants slow arteriosclerosis in the hearts of people who have not had heart transplants.

STATIN DRUGS

If you've got high levels of cholesterol and CRP, and aspirin didn't get the levels down, you might be a candidate for one of the popular cholesterol-lowering drugs known as "statins" (for the ending of their chemical names). Statins include fluvastatin (Lescol), atorvastatin (Lipitor), lovastatin (Mevacor), pravastatin (Pravachol), and simvastatin (Zocor).

Statins are a type of cholesterol-reducing drug that lowers the levels of fats in the blood, including cholesterol and triglycerides.

Other types of cholesterol-lowering drugs include fibrates, bile acid resins, and nicotinic acid. Although all these drugs are commonly used to treat high cholesterol, statins are considered the first line of treatment for patients with this condition.

Research has shown that statins not only help reduce inflammation and cholesterol but also may lower CRP levels. Although many patients seem to be unusually concerned about the safety of statins for some reason, cholesterol-lowering statins are in fact remarkably safe and effective. Tens of millions of Americans are taking them every day without problems.

Researchers are currently studying how beneficial statin drugs can be in reducing cardiovascular risk in people with normal cholesterol levels but high CRP levels—a group that currently lacks generally accepted treatment options.

Paul Ridker, M.D., the world's leading expert on CRP, is currently conducting a 3½-year study with fifteen thousand patients to see if the statin drug rosuvastatin (Crestor) can cut the risk of serious heart problems among patients with high levels of CRP.

The trial is enrolling men over age fifty-five and women over age sixty-five who have LDL cholesterol under 130 and a CRP score over 2 (a moderate to high risk). Half of the patients will get 20 milligrams a day of Crestor; the other half will get a placebo. The drug has not yet been approved for marketing in the United States.

Another study found that it took longer for patients' diabetes to get worse if they were taking statins. In fact, those patients who used statins needed insulin nearly a year later than those who didn't take statins. Previous studies have shown that people who take statins have a 33 percent lower risk of developing diabetes.

Side Effects

Statin drugs are remarkably safe. While there is the potential for liver irritation, this can be detected during routine blood testing after the drug is started. There also have been some reports of muscle irritation that stops when the drug is withdrawn. More serious cases of muscle breakdown can occur, especially when a statin drug is used with other cholesterol-lowering agents. Despite these possibilities, experience with more than 100 million prescriptions has proven these drugs to be quite safe.

BETA-BLOCKERS

Beta-blockers are used to treat high blood pressure, congestive heart failure, abnormal heart rhythms, and chest pain. They also can be used to prevent future heart attacks in patients at risk. These drugs work by blocking the effects of adrenaline on your body's beta receptors, slowing the nerve impulses traveling through the heart. As a result, your heart does not have to work as hard, because it needs less blood and oxygen. Beta-blockers also block the impulses that can cause disturbed heart rhythms.

Your body has two main beta receptors (beta 1 and beta 2). Some beta-blockers block beta 1 receptors (responsible for heart rate and strength) more than they block beta 2 receptors (responsible for the function of muscles over which you have no control). Nonselective beta-blockers block both beta 1 and beta 2 receptors.

While taking beta-blockers, you should not eat or drink anything that contains caffeine or take over-the-counter cough and cold medicines, antihistamines, or antacids that contain aluminum. You also should avoid drinking alcohol, which can decrease the effects of beta-blockers. There are many beta-blockers available, but the most common are nadolol (Corgard), atenolol (Tenormin), metoprolol (Lopressor), and propranolol (Inderal).

Side Effects

As with any medication, beta-blockers have the potential for side effects. Common side effects include fatigue, cold hands and feet, weakness or dizziness, and dry mouth, eyes, and skin. Less common side effects include wheezing, trouble breathing, or shortness of breath; slow heartbeat; trouble sleeping or vivid dreams while asleep; and swelling. Beta blockers can trigger asthma attacks in patients with asthma. Not uncommonly, patients report decreased libido when taking these medications. At high doses, beta blockers may lower the beneficial HDL cholesterol as well as raise triglycerides. Rare side effects include cramps, vomiting, diarrhea, constipation, back or joint pain, skin rash, sore throat, depression, memory loss, confusion, and hallucinations. Tell your doctor right away if you have any of these side effects, but *don't stop taking the medication unless your doctor tells you to.* If you stop taking your medicine abruptly without the help of your physician, you may experience a significant rebound effect of high blood pressure, fast heart rate, severe angina, and even heart attack.

ACE INHIBITORS

ACE inhibitors lower blood pressure and are commonly prescribed to treat high blood pressure. They generally begin to affect the body within one to two hours after being taken by mouth and almost instantly after injection. Here's how they work: Everyone has some amount of angiotensin I in their blood. It's converted to angiotensin II (a substance that causes blood vessels to tighten, increasing blood pressure) by an enzyme in your body called angiotensin converting enzyme (ACE). When you take an ACE inhibitor, it blocks ACE, thereby preventing angiotensin I from being converted into angiotensin II. Reducing angiotensin II lets your blood vessels relax and expand, lowering blood pressure. Relaxing the arteries also helps to improve the pumping efficiency of a failing heart, boosting cardiac output in patients with heart failure. Many medical studies over the

last twenty years show ACE inhibitors reducing the risk of death from congestive heart failure by 20 to 40 percent. ACE inhibitors are used to treat both high
blood pressure and congestive heart failure. Current ACE inhibitors include
benazepril (Lotensin), captopril (Capoten), lisinopril (Zestril, Prinivil), quinapril
(Accupril), and ramipril (Altace).

Side Effects

The most common side effect of ACE inhibitors is coughing, which is not
serious. You'll need to take occasional blood tests to screen for an abnormally
high level of potassium in the blood, a potentially serious side effect.

CALCIUM CHANNEL BLOCKERS

Calcium channel blockers are used to treat chest pain or high blood pressure.
They work by letting more blood flow to the heart muscle and relaxing the
blood vessels, so the blood flows more easily through your body. Patients diagnosed with high blood pressure are often given a calcium channel blocker to
reduce cardiovascular disease risk, but the benefit compared with other drug
classes is controversial. Calcium channel blockers include bepridil (Vascor),
diltiazem (Cardizem), felodipine (Plendil), isradipine (Dynacirc), nicardipine
(Cardene), nifedipine (Procardia), nisoldipine (Sular), and verapamil (Calan).

Side Effects

Side effects vary greatly, depending on the type and dosage of calcium channel blocker prescribed. They include dizziness, abnormally slow or fast heartbeat, low blood pressure, heart block, fatigue, and shortness of breath. And
in one 1995 study comparing patients with high blood pressure, those taking
short-acting calcium channel blockers experienced a 60 percent increase in
heart attack compared to those treated with other blood pressure medications.
This problem has not been evident in long-acting calcium blockers. A 2000
study also found that patients taking calcium channel blockers had a significantly higher risk of heart attack and congestive heart failure.

NITROGLYCERIN

Nitroglycerin dilates blood vessels and is often used to manage chest pain (angina). Synthesized in 1846, nitroglycerin was first used to treat angina in 1879 and was granted FDA approval in 1938. Nitroglycerin is a vasodilator, relaxing the blood vessels and reducing the pumping force the heart must exert to circulate blood through the body. This relieves the crushing pain of angina, which is caused by a lack of oxygen to the heart muscle.

Although the classic method of taking nitroglycerin is to place a tablet under the tongue to allow the drug to dissolve, these days we tend to use the spray form of the drug because it has a much longer shelf life. Nitro tablets lose their effectiveness within about six months, but the spray form lasts two to three years. Be sure to sit or lie down when taking nitroglycerin, because the drug will lower your blood pressure so quickly you could faint.

If you have persistent chest pain after three sprays five minutes apart, you should call 911, because the pain may indicate you're having a heart attack, or unstable angina.

Side Effects

Nitroglycerin most often causes headaches (and low blood pressure, as already mentioned), but it also may cause insomnia, flushing, restlessness, or nightmares.

IN THE NEXT CHAPTER

While diet, exercise, and lifestyle changes can help lower CRP levels and improve cardiovascular health, sometimes medication is required to make a difference. When all else fails, you may need to consider surgery. In the next chapter, we'll briefly outline your options.

9

Surgery: What You
Need to Know

Living a healthy lifestyle and taking medication can help prevent blocked
arteries from worsening—and if blockages don't worsen, they won't hurt
you. The preceding chapters discuss the very important issues of diet, exercise, and lifestyle and how they interact to discourage blockage from progressing with time.

BEYOND LIFESTYLE MODIFICATION AND MEDICATION

We used to think blockage would grow steadily over time under the influence
of uncontrolled blood pressure, high cholesterol, nicotine, and heredity. We now
know this is not the case. Blockage can remain unchanged for many years and
then suddenly get worse. It may grow substantially and stop, or grow rapidly
and close the vessel, stopping all blood flow until a heart attack occurs. Once a
heart attack occurs, one-third of all patients will not survive the next two hours.

From microscopically examining the arteries of those who have died, we
now have a better understanding of what goes wrong when a heart attack
occurs. Under stable conditions where a blockage is not quickly getting worse,
there is a thick layer of tissue on the surface of the blockage. Think of this as
a band-aid that keeps the material in the blockage from contacting the flowing blood. This is the body's attempt to wall off the problem—and the thicker
the band-aid, the better.

This is important, since the material *within* that blockage rapidly promotes
blood clotting. Under the microscope, we can see a special type of white blood

cells in this band-aid that secrete chemicals that erode the fibrous cap. If enough erosion occurs, the band-aid breaks and the material inside the blockage come in contact with the circulating blood. The body recognizes this as a crisis and comes to the "rescue." The body thinks there is a hole in the blood vessel, (which there is) and forms a blood clot.

It is perfectly appropriate for your body to do this if you cut your finger, but it often turns out to be a lethal miscue when it's your heart artery that is involved.

Those cells that produce these chemicals are inflammatory cells, broadly termed *chemical mediators of inflammation*. This is why the measurement of CRP is so important. CRP detects inflammation, and inflammation is the key underlying process that leads to blockage growth. We now believe that when inflammation is under control (and CRP is low) blockage remains stable and doesn't grow. When inflammation occurs (and CRP rises) the fibrous cap can erode—which can be catastrophic.

A complete vessel blockage and heart attack is the ultimate end-point of the inflammatory process. Most researchers believe that the process of inflammation smolders on an ongoing basis. Microscopically, we can see rings within the blockage, like the rings of a tree, which represents scars from previous "battles" with inflammation.

The human body is rich with systems of checks and balances that can counteract damage such as blockage growth. Those checks and balances, however, are balanced precariously between healing and causing premature cardiac death.

ANGIOPLASTY AND STENTING

Previous chapters have discussed details of diet, exercise, and stress reduction in detail. Although these are not procedures or prescriptions, they are very powerful in their ability to reduce the chances of progressive blockage disease.

Our health is a product of the genes we inherited from our parents and our lifestyle. We can change our nurture, but we cannot trade in our genes for better ones. Accordingly, despite our best efforts, sometimes things can go horribly wrong. Sometimes a person experiences rapid blockage that interferes with blood flow—what we call an "acute coronary syndrome." This is usually, but not always, associated with symptoms.

The typical symptoms are that of a dull, burning, pressure-like tightness in the chest area that might radiate into the left arm, neck, or jaw. This is typically brought on by activity or emotional upset and is relieved by rest. It might be associated with shortness of breath and/or sweatiness. Occasionally (especially in women), the symptoms are less typical. Often there may simply be breathlessness with activity; at times, there may be complete absence of symptoms. Symptoms are especially worrisome if they occur with increasing frequency, severity, or duration.

Patients who have unstable heart symptoms are often best treated by aggressive methods, such as fixing blood vessels through a catheter. In this procedure, a doctor places an IV into the artery near the hip and then inserts a small plastic tube through the IV, up the main blood vessel of the body (the aorta). Since there are no nerves on the inside of the blood vessels, the person does not feel any of this. An x-ray dye is then injected (called a *heart catheterization*) to identify the blocked area of the artery, and a small balloon or a wire mesh device called a *stent* is used to widen the narrowed area within the artery, permitting the blood to flow freely (called a *percutanious coronary intervention,* or PCI).

Although it is clear that an aggressive, invasive approach like this creates better results for patients with unstable symptoms, it is less clear whether this helps patients without symptoms or whose lesions are stable. In stable patients with chest discomfort, a stent can reduce the amount of chest pain they experience, but there is not a dramatic drop in their risk of heart attack or sudden death. For this reason, stable patients are best treated with lifestyle improvements, including exercise as appropriate, stress reduction, and medications that research has shown are helpful, such as statins.

HEART BYPASS SURGERY

Occasionally so much blockage is found—or blockage is found in certain places such as the branch points or the left main coronary artery—that coronary artery bypass grafting (CABG) is recommended. At times, it is quite clear CABG is the best option. At other times, it is less clear whether bypass surgery, stent placement, or medical treatment is best.

This is when it helps to have a good idea about the kind of doctor you're working with. Since cardiologists perform the catheterization, the type of cardiologist that performs the procedure may well influence the recommended procedure. In other words, conservative physicians may opt for a conservative course of medical treatment, whereas others may be concerned enough to want to do something but may not be aggressive enough to try to fix the blockage with techniques using a catheter, such as stents, angioplasty, or other similar methods. These physicians may suggest open-heart surgery as a default approach. The best physician will carefully weigh all the variables and recommend what they would want for their own Mom or Dad in the same situation.

After heart surgery, blockage may form in the bypasses or the vessels into which the bypasses attach. Bypasses are of two types, arteries and veins. Typically an artery off the inside of the chest wall is redirected to the heart. Since this vessel may supply one or at most two vessels, veins from the leg may be used to bypass other blood vessels. Patients who have this type of surgery but don't make lifestyle changes expose themselves to continued risk of blood vessel damage and blockage formation. Those who change all they can change and live a prudent cardiac lifestyle minimize their risk of new disease after bypass surgery.

It is important to remember that *heart surgery doesn't cure anything*. It simply bypasses the blocked arteries. Unless the individual changes the cause of the problem in the first place—such as diet or lifestyle—the same potential for progressive disease still exists.

The best outcome after heart surgery occurs when the patient realizes all the things they can control—weight, blood pressure, blood sugar, blood cholesterol, and how much they exercise. If a person takes control of all these variables, their outcome improves. Most of these variables are in the patient's hands—not doctors, hospitals, or pharmacies.

Heart surgery, like all other areas of medicine, continues to undergo dramatic progress. We now know that less frequent use of the bypass pump, smaller incisions, and the ability to treat older and sicker patients translates into better outcomes.

Remember that not all heart surgery is the same. You must understand not only the individual heart surgeon's expertise, but also that of the hospital where the surgeon works. Volume matters. Hospitals that treat only a few cases with your problem may not be the best place to have heart surgery.

To a person with a hammer, everything looks like a nail that needs pounding. This seems to be the work ethic of mediocre surgeons. Good heart surgeons will not routinely operate without careful thought on patients referred to them. Instead, good surgeons will weigh the risks and benefits of all the treatment options for the individual patient, and sometimes recommend an alternative treatment.

Depending upon the state, outcome data for individual surgeons and hospitals may be a matter of public record and are often reported in the newspaper. A good reporting system will also include information on how sick the patients are who undergo surgery; this must be considered when evaluating the surgeon's or hospital's statistics. Time spent investigating the available information is invaluable.

Sadly, competent and well-trained doctors are getting harder to find. It's even rarer to find someone who has the time to spend with you to address all your concerns, fully explain the diagnosis, and put your fears to rest. Owing to the constraints of modern health care and insurance issues, none of us has as much time as we would wish to spend with our patients.

The result: people are starved for information. If they're facing a serious condition like heart disease, they're scared. They feel alone, overwhelmed, intimidated. Yet doctors today find there's barely enough time to make the crucial medical decisions that have to be made, let alone worry about how a patient's emotional state and quality of life are faring. And yet that can be the key to survival itself.

By empowering yourself with the following information, you'll be in a much better position to take responsibility for your own health care.

Finding a Cardiologist

You can find a cardiologist the typical way, by asking family and friends or getting a referral from your family doctor. Or you can go online and check out the backgrounds of hundreds of cardiologists (for a small fee) by using one of several pay-as-you-go search engines. Or visit HeartCenterOnline (heartcenteronline.com) and try their Physician Finder, which allows you to search by physician name or by practices closest to you. You can also refine your search by specialty, gender, or specific conditions, tests, or procedures.

BEFORE YOUR APPOINTMENT

If you suspect you have heart problems or if your CRP and lipid tests have come back with questionable or high levels, you'll need to meet with a cardiologist. A little preparation can help you make the most of the upcoming appointment.

A few days before your appointment, make a list of your symptoms so you can describe them clearly—including the frequency and time they occur and how they feel. Make a note of any past treatments you've had. Now write down all of your questions and concerns and bring the list along with you to the appointment. Your list will probably include the following questions:

- Are my symptoms serious?
- What can I expect from this visit?
- Will my insurance pay for this visit?
- Are there strategies I can do at home that may improve my heart risk?

It's common for people to suddenly think of unasked questions right after leaving a doctor's office. Writing those questions down in advance, and even handing the list to the cardiologist, can help ensure that all of your questions will be addressed. You'll also want to make a list of all drug allergies and a list of all the drugs you're currently taking.

If you haven't already done so, call the doctor's office a day or two before your appointment to find out how long the appointment is likely to take and which tests you can expect to take. If you were not given specific instructions when the appointment was made, ask if it will be important to stop eating or drinking before any blood work is to be done. I once had a patient who drank a big glass of orange juice right before having blood drawn; his blood sugar skyrocketed because of the juice, throwing the office into a panic—they thought he had a blood sugar problem.

AT THE DOCTOR'S OFFICE

Arrive at the doctor's office with your list of notes and symptom diaries. You might want to bring along a spouse, family member, or friend—someone who can help you remember everything the doctor tells you. Most doctors today have only a limited amount of time for an office visit, so it pays to be organized and on time.

Here's what to do during the first visit:

- Describe your symptoms, including when they started, how often they occur, and if they are getting worse.
- Take notes.
- Be sure you understand what the cardiologist says, and ask for explanations of anything you don't understand.
- If the doctor prescribes medications, make sure you understand the instructions, such as when to take the drug, what to do if you forget a dose, what food or other drugs to avoid while taking this medicine, and what side effects may occur.
- If you think you'll have trouble following the treatment regimen the doctor is advocating, say so right away.

Screening Recommendations

The American Heart Association recommends that physicians routinely assess patients' general risk of cardiovascular disease beginning at age twenty.

Every Two Years
Doctors should perform these tests:

- blood pressure
- body mass index (BMI)
- waist circumference
- pulse

Every Five Years
Doctors should perform these tests:

- cholesterol profile
- glucose levels

Physicians should calculate the ten-year risk of developing cardiovascular disease for

- people age forty and older
- people with multiple heart disease risk factors

TESTS

At the doctor's office, you'll probably be given a cardiovascular exam, which is far more focused on the condition and function of the heart and blood vessels than a more general physical. You can expect your doctor to listen to your heart, lungs, and blood vessels through a stethoscope, checking for crackling sounds in the lungs (rales) that could signify lung congestion or congestive heart failure. A heart murmur could be a sign of diseased valves. A sound called a *bruit* in the carotid artery in the neck could be a sign of carotid artery disease, increasing your risk of stroke.

In addition to listening through the stethoscope, the health care professional will also use a finger or two to lightly press the area over certain arteries and veins to feel the blood flowing just beneath the skin. Any weakened or abnormal pulse in any part of the body could be a possible sign of heart-related disease. Your doctor may use a bright light to examine your eyes, checking the health of the tiny blood vessels that are vulnerable to damage or disease from diabetes.

If any unusual symptoms are observed during the preliminary exam, or just to rule out heart disease, your doctor may order special tests in addition to blood tests to assess the strength and health of your heart. These include:

- *EKG* This simple recording of your heart's electrical activity can pinpoint abnormal heartbeats, blood flow problems, muscle damage, and heart enlargement.
- *Holter monitor* Because everyday stress can affect your heart's rhythm, this device can measure how well your heart works as you go about your daily life. If you've noticed very fast or slow heartbeats, irregular beats, or palpitations, your cardiologist might suggest a Holter monitor. You'll wear a small EKG recording device for twenty-four hours to find out how well your heart responds to daily stress.
- *Treadmill (stress) test* Because some heart problems only become obvious as the heart is stressed, the treadmill test pairs an EKG with exercise (either on a treadmill or an exercise bike). This test is safe when performed under medical supervision; if you experience any discomfort, the test will be stopped. (Keep in mind that the classic treadmill test used to diagnose potential heart disease isn't as accurate in diagnosing coronary artery disease in women as it is in men.)
- *Stress echocardiography* In this test, you'll exercise while a device uses sound waves to create pictures of your heart, revealing heart motion

and your response to stress. It is much more accurate than a treadmill test for women, although it is more expensive.

- *Ultrafast CT scan* This high-speed CAT scan takes multiple cross-section images of your heart during a single heartbeat, providing much more detail about the heart's function and structures while greatly decreasing the amount of time required for a test. It can detect very small amounts of calcium in the heart and coronary arteries that may indicate the beginnings of lesions that could one day cause a blockage or heart attack. This state-of-the-art method can help predict future heart problems in people as young as forty or fifty, even if there is no other sign of cardiovascular disease.
- *Nuclear scan* This test measures heart muscle contractions as blood flows through the heart, using a radioactive material injected into a vein and scanned with a camera. Sluggish blood flow during exercise could indicate narrowed blood vessels of the heart.
- *Coronary angiography* Also known as cardiac catheterization, this test checks for blocked arteries by threading a thin plastic tube through the arteries of the heart and injecting x-ray dye to better visualize the internal lining of the blood vessel.
- *Cardiac MRI* Magnetic resonance imaging (MRI) uses sophisticated computer technology and magnetic fields as a noninvasive way to check for blockage.
- *Carotid medial thickness* This ultrasound examination of the neck arteries is a way to check for increased thickness of the neck artery, which correlates to heart artery blockage.

If You Need a Test

Patients complaining of heart symptoms are often given a battery of tests to pinpoint the problem. If your doctor wants you to have a test, ask:

- Why is the test recommended?
- What can we learn from it?
- What are the risks and benefits?
- Are there any less invasive tests that could provide the same information?
- Should I do anything differently before the test (such as make any changes in eating/drinking or medications)?

- What will happen during the test?
- How long will the test take?
- How should I prepare for it?
- Will I be able to drive home afterward?
- Should I bring someone with me?
- Will there be any side effects?
- Will there be any pain?
- When will the results be ready?
- Depending on what the test finds, what will happen afterward?
- How long will the recovery period last?
- Will my insurance company cover this test?

Getting the Test Results

There are new questions to write down and ask the cardiologist once the results are in. Here are some important questions to ask:

- What did the test show?
- What were my exact values, and what is the normal range for other people my age?
- What do the terms in this report mean?
- Is more testing necessary? If so, which tests are needed and why?
- What is my diagnosis and possible treatments (including experimental treatments)?
- Could this condition have been prevented?
- Will the condition get worse?
- Did I inherit this condition?
- Should my family be tested for this condition?

IF A PROCEDURE IS RECOMMENDED

Very often, a cardiologist might recommend an invasive procedure to diagnose or treat a heart problem. You should be prepared ahead of time for this possibility and bring this list of questions to the doctor's office:

- Why are you recommending this procedure?
- Are there any risks associated with it?
- Are there any less invasive procedures that would be just as beneficial?
- Exactly how is the procedure performed?
- Will there be pain?
- Will I need an anesthetic?
- How long will the procedure take?
- Should I bring someone with me, and will I be able to drive myself home?
- Is it possible to have this procedure as an outpatient?
- Should I eat or drink differently before the procedure or change the way I take my medications?
- Will further treatment be necessary?
- How soon can I lift heavy objects, climb stairs, and go back to work after this procedure?
- How soon can I have sex after this procedure?
- Will my insurance cover this procedure?

After the Procedure

After the procedure has been successfully completed, your cardiologist will sit down with you and discuss your situation. This is the time to bring out the next list of questions:

- Was the procedure successful?
- Did you find anything unusual during the procedure?
- Will I ever need to have that procedure again?
- How soon can I return to regular daily activities?
- What side effects should I call you about?
- Will I be taking any new medications? If so, how should I take them, and what side effects can I expect?
- What should I do if I notice side effects—get immediate emergency medical help or simply make an appointment to see you again?

EVOLVING TECHNOLOGY

A few years ago, angioplasty was the only method (short of open-heart surgery) of opening blood flow within a blocked artery. Stents became available in 1994; this reduced the risk that scar tissue would return from about 35 percent to 15 percent. In May 2003, the FDA approved stents impregnated with medication that discourages scar tissue formation. This has reduced scar tissue formation from 15 percent to approximately 4 percent. Scar tissue recurrence is one of the reasons heart surgery is performed. This technology will continue to improve and may affect the frequency with which patients are referred to heart surgery.

CRP AND THE FUTURE

As medical science advances and more physicians become comfortable with the powerful prognostic ability of CRP, such knowledge will be incorporated in helping define the best care. Currently, CRP remains a hot area of research. Data will help determine what medications and procedures will work best based in part on CRP levels.

IN THE NEXT CHAPTER

Now that you've learned all you can about the role CRP plays in your heart's health and all of the different lifestyle changes you can make to lower your CRP levels, it's time to think about putting all the information together in forming a plan for the rest of your life. That's what we'll do in the next chapter, where I'll give you a peek into the ways a cardiologist approaches a heart-healthy future.

10

Putting It All Together

So now you know the basics. But what are you going to do *today*, in light of all this information, to lower your chance of a life cut short by heart disease? That is what this chapter is all about. Together we're going to construct a game plan based on solid scientific data to help you do the best you can to live well.

First, I want you to put this book down. Go get yourself an enjoyable beverage—perhaps a hot mug of black tea with very real heart-healthy benefits! A glass of red wine comes to mind as well (but perhaps at the end of this chapter). Curl up in a comfortable place, perhaps with soft background music, and we'll begin. (As I write this, I'm listening to the beautiful piano of Michael Jones.)

Congratulations, you've already taken the first step in our game plan! By getting yourself a "comfort beverage" and locating a special place to relax, you're taking care of yourself. You're pampering yourself. This isn't indulgent; it's a critically important step in the right direction.

YOUR EMOTIONAL HEALTH

You must be interested in your own health and well-being, because it's the foundation of successful healthy living. It might seem quite obvious to you, but the actions of so many people I see every day in my office suggest otherwise.

Each of us follows a unique path through life. Some grow up in loving, nurturing environments, but many of us come from a past where something was lacking. There are often unmet needs we struggle with; like an itch we can't quite scratch to satisfaction, some of us are left unfulfilled. Unknowingly, we try to fill that void with things, superficial relationships, unhealthy substances, or the numbing tonic of overwork.

Eventually, there comes a point when the emotionally deprived among us realize—either consciously or subconsciously—that those unmet needs from childhood cannot be so easily fixed. Survivors get counseling, reach an understanding, and move on. Nonsurvivors never make it that far. People stuck in that bleak place lack a sense of perspective and purpose, and their own health is the farthest thing from their mind. This is one reason why so many people continue to smoke despite knowing the negative effect nicotine will have on the quality and quantity of their life. Solace is taken in small bites, with frequent trips to the refrigerator or the liquor store. Time and disease march on and take their toll.

Think about eating. How often are we truly hungry when we eat? I've asked patients to keep a "consumption journal," logging their entire food intake over a two-week period. I also ask them to indicate, on a scale of one to four, how hungry they were each time they ate. It's remarkable to see the difference in how much they eat between the first week and the second week. It doesn't take long before patients quickly realize, "I'm not that hungry. I'll eat less." I typically see a 5- to 10-pound weight loss with that simple trick.

Issues of emotions and eating are intimately related. As infants, we often experienced the most direct love and affection during mealtimes. We were held, sung to, and kissed throughout our entire meal. When was the last time that's happened to you? It's no wonder we look for comfort in food as an adult.

If you're in a similar lonely place, help is available. Most locales have "Samaritan centers" that can provide counseling, often at little or no cost. I've seen many patients who—once they confronted their issues—were able to rise above them and deal very effectively with their physical health issues. Remember, there isn't any magical separation between your mind and your body. Let there be no mistake about this: a well-led life begins with making sure the emotional foundation is solid.

As you start on your journey toward better health, stop for a moment and assess your current situation. If you're remarkably overweight or you smoke, do you have any emotional issues you're struggling with? I'd encourage you to speak to your physician about your concerns. Your primary care provider or cardiologist can refer you to a therapist skilled in dealing with these issues.

Sadly, modern medicine often fails to adequately address and treat this important emotional aspect of human health. When issues of emotional health are adequately treated, patients find an inner peace that fuels their ability to overcome negative lifestyle choices such as poor diet, lack of exercise, or smoking.

A WORD ABOUT BLOOD PRESSURE

Kendra was a twenty-seven-year-old newly married woman who came to my office to find out why she needed more and more blood pressure pills to control her spiraling blood pressure. At the time, Kendra was taking four different medications, and she was concerned about the impact of these pills on her long-term health. She seemed to develop side effects from most medications, and her daily stress levels were sky-high.

In an attempt to reduce the number of pills she was swallowing each day, Kendra enrolled in a yoga and meditation class offered by the local hospital. She was a highly motivated young woman, and with the help of this program, Kendra reported a dramatic reduction in her stress level. Her sleep habits improved, and soon she needed fewer and fewer drugs. Today she only takes one low-dose diuretic.

The latest statistics suggest that 30 percent of Americans don't realize that they have high blood pressure, less than 60 percent with hypertension are getting treatment, and only about one-third have their hypertension under good control. Even modest increases in blood pressure can double the risk of heart disease and strokes.

What Is High Blood Pressure?

High blood pressure affects about one out of every four adult Americans, and it's especially common among African Americans, who develop the problem earlier than Caucasians. Age is another strong risk factor; even people with perfectly normal blood pressure at age fifty-five have a 90 percent lifetime risk for developing hypertension.

Blood pressure is the force of blood against artery walls, and it's recorded as two numbers—systolic pressure (as the heart beats) over diastolic pressure (as the heart relaxes between beats). Both numbers are important.

Blood pressure rises and falls during the day. When it remains high over time, it's called hypertension, and it's dangerous because it forces the heart to work too hard. This strongly pulsing blood flow can harm arteries. Unfortunately, high blood pressure often has no warning signs or symptoms, and once it develops, it usually lasts a lifetime.

New Guidelines

You may have read that the new guidelines have been introduced in which a blood pressure of 120/80 is now considered "prehypertension." This new category recognizes the fact that even small increases in blood pressure carry some added risk and that people whose blood pressure reaches this cutoff are at increased risk for developing full-fledged hypertension in the future.

While many people focus on their diastolic blood pressure reading (the "bottom" number), the systolic blood pressure ("top" number) is much better at predicting who is at risk for heart attacks, strokes, and heart failure. This is particularly true for those over fifty. Although most people need treatment only when their blood pressure is greater than 140/90, those folks who thought they were perfectly healthy at 120/80 are now wondering what to do about their heart.

Fortunately, lifestyle changes can play an important role in keeping blood pressure under control. Regular exercise, weight loss, and healthy diets can lower blood pressure by as much as 10 to 20 points. When lifestyle changes don't work, your doctor may turn to medications to lower your hypertension.

But the treatment prescribed by a doctor can only work if patients are motivated to take their medications, make lifestyle changes, and visit their doctor regularly. Finding ways to motivate patients remains a key area for improvement.

What You Can Do

Be sure to have your blood pressure checked regularly; millions of Americans have no idea their blood pressure is too high. Most adults should have their blood pressure checked at least once every one to two years. But don't wait to see your doctor; you can easily have your blood pressure checked at a local pharmacy, gym, or health clinic. If your blood pressure is any higher than 130/85, tell your health care provider and consider making some lifestyle changes, such as

- losing weight (see Chapter 4)
- following a low-salt diet like the DASH plan (see Chapter 4)
- limiting alcohol to no more than one or two drinks a day

- getting regular exercise (thirty minutes most days of the week)
- quitting smoking

Recent studies suggest these lifestyle changes can prevent as well as treat the first stages of high blood pressure. If you are already being treated for high blood pressure, you can make your treatment more effective by

- learning more about your condition
- taking your medications every day
- monitoring your blood pressure at home
- visiting your doctor regularly
- getting more serious about lifestyle changes

Here are some natural ways to prevent or reduce high blood pressure:

- *Stop smoking* Not only will this help keep your blood pressure in line, but you'll also diminish your risk of cancer, stroke, and cardiovascular diseases. If you smoke, you're two to six times more likely to suffer a heart attack, and the risk increases with the number of cigarettes you smoke each day. The nicotine in a single cigarette is strong enough to boost blood pressure levels above normal, and it will be thirty to sixty minutes before blood pressure returns to normal.
- *Lose weight* The more overweight you are, the higher your risk of developing high blood pressure. Start by cutting just 200 to 300 calories from your diet each day—the equivalent of saying no to a piece of chocolate cake.
- *Decrease salt intake* Consume no more than about a teaspoon of salt a day (2,000 milligrams of sodium). The average American gets twice that amount, often hidden in processed foods. Add more fruits, vegetables, and low-fat dairy products.
- *Limit alcohol* Any more than one or two drinks a day will increase blood pressure.
- *Exercise* Slowly begin aerobic exercise (with your doctor's okay), increasing the time and intensity. Aim for at least a thirty-minute workout most days of the week.

PLAN YOUR DAY

Now it's time to plan. What goals, based on what science has taught us, do we want to achieve? We want to eat correctly, exercise some, and reduce stress. Reduce stress? Impossible, you say? You already have the tools; I'll show you how to use them.

Let me take you through a typical day that achieves these goals. For me, morning has special meaning and importance. I was at one time convinced I could never be a "morning person." Then, some time ago, I sat down with a cup of tea to take stock and create a plan to live better. I decided to give early morning a try. I was pleasantly surprised how easy it was.

Early Morning

My wife and I have three children—the oldest is thirteen and the youngest is three. On school days, the oldest gets up at 6:15 A.M. with minimal prodding, but our youngest is up around 7 A.M. and needs a lot of supervision. I've found the time before our youngest gets up to be rewarding and productive— and it's mine, all mine!

My alarm rings at 4:30 A.M. Absurd? Inhumane? Read on, and you'll see I'm being rather self-indulgent. I need about a half hour to wake up. The coffee brews, the cobwebs fade. I often push paper on my desk. (I don't like piles.) Then I have two hours to do exactly what I want. For at least thirty minutes a day, and sixty minutes every other day, I exercise.

I've made exercise fun, so that I actually look forward to it. If the weather is nice, I take a brisk walk in the predawn light. The world is still and peaceful. If the weather keeps me indoors, I spend time on a treadmill in the basement. I walk at 4.2 miles per hour at a 10 percent grade; I don't run because it's too much strain on the knees. I can watch continuing medical education videotapes or a videotape of David Letterman from the night before. When I am done, I feel great. I'm invigorated, fully alert, and ready to take on the world's problems.

In this way, I've taken the time to pay attention to myself first. Selfish? Not at all. If I'm sidelined with a heart attack, how am I helping my family? Taking care of myself is a very important responsibility to my wife and family. It's a fact: physical activity makes people live longer. I need to be there for my family, so by exercising first thing, no matter how long my day becomes or how physically or emotionally draining it is, I've gotten in my exercise.

I highly recommend a morning approach to exercise, because it's the only sure way to get it done. We all know how the day can evolve and how spent we often feel toward the end of the day. It's a lot easier to not exercise at the end of the day. Be good to yourself. Take care of yourself first.

If you haven't engaged in a formal exercise program, it's important to discuss this with your physician. He or she may consider some risk evaluation prior to giving you the green light. Remember, the type of exercise need not be akin to marine boot camp training. A simple walking program is very reasonable. Start off slow and ultimately aim for a brisk, nonstop walk for thirty to forty minutes daily.

Within a week of starting your exercise program, you'll notice something unusual. In response to exercise, your brain produces a chemical called beta-endorphin that is chemically similar to morphine. Beta-endorphin gives you a strong sense of well-being, but it lacks the negative features of its narcotic cousin. Beta-endorphin is only produced when you continue to exercise. Runners who are injured and are unable to exercise become quite cranky, probably because of withdrawal from beta-endorphin.

Beta-endorphin, by virtue of its ability to confer a sense of well-being, also helps you achieve goals such as smoking abstinence and weight maintenance. There is no downside to beta-endorphin. The important point to understand, however, is that it's produced in the brain *only* after exercise.

The Morning Meal

After morning exercise and a shower, it's time to eat. *Never* skip breakfast. If you don't take in calories on a routine basis, your body's metabolism starts to slow down, which slows the rate at which calories are burned.

Breakfast is a time for fruit and grains, although the specifics are up to you. For me, a multigrain bagel or oatmeal fits the bill. I use Benecol spread on my bagel—that's a great-tasting alternative to butter or margarine that contains plant stanol esters with a proven ability to lower cholesterol. A banana and glass of orange juice round out the meal, and I'm set for the day. As I leave for the hospital, I pack my "secret weapon" for midmorning hunger attacks.

The Work Day

Whether you work at home or outside the home, work is still work. My wife is a family physician who has chosen to stay home with our young child. In many ways her job is a lot more difficult than mine. Although I take care of the dinner dishes most of the time, the work of the house still remains throughout the day. Her time on and off the job is blurred by living where she works. When I leave the hospital, unless I'm on call, I'm done. I feel the relief of leaving one place and going home where I am greeted warmly (at least by a three-year-old!). It is an enjoyable feeling. Those temporal and geographical distinctions are lacking for a stay-at-home mom. While I am often thanked profusely several times throughout my professional day for doing my job, my wife struggles to potty train our three-year-old without any pats on the back for a tough job well done.

It's important for us as a couple to keep proper perspective on this "big picture." My wife has decided to stay at home to remain in our children's lives as much a possible, and she's made tremendous professional sacrifices to do this. I deeply appreciate the sacrifices she's made.

Throughout our daily life, it's easy to lose sight of the big picture. What I like to call the *therapeutic sense of perspective* is very helpful to think about many times during the day. Does your present concern really deserve attention, or have you lost sight of the big picture? Remember, you can't have a bad day unless you allow it to happen. We all have our trials and stresses of daily life. How we react to them is up to us.

I'm Hungry!

With remarkable predictability, my stomach tells me its 10:30 A.M. I'm hungry. It's time for my secret weapon—those peeled, tiny, ready-to-eat carrots. The ultimate "fast-food," these can be eaten on the run without preparation, and you don't have to worry about dripping "special sauce" on your shirt. High in fiber and vitamins, these little wonders fill me up and tide me over until lunch. Six tall glasses of water throughout the day serve to curb my appetite (check with your doctor about drinking this much water if you have a history of congestive heart failure).

At lunch I choose a salad with the dressing on the side. I dip my fork in the dressing and then the salad; this way, I have dressing on each forkful, but when I'm finished with the salad, the bulk of the dressing is still in the container, not in me, potentially clogging my arteries. I'll save my dessert—usually an apple—for midafternoon.

By the end of the day, I'm heading home, having consumed about 650 calories. Had I started my day with a stop at McDonald's for a Spanish omelet bagel (710 calories) and hash browns (130 calories) and then returned at lunch for a Big Mac (590 calories), large fries (540 calories), and a medium coke (210 calories), I would have consumed approximately 2,180 calories.

If your daily food intake reads a lot like that, it's easy to see how easily the numbers can add up, contributing to the fact that 60 percent of the U.S. population is considered overweight or obese.

Day's End

I enjoy arriving home as dinner preparations begin. I get the opportunity to reconnect with my wife while we work together in the kitchen. She and I could exist on an exclusive diet of fresh grilled salmon or black beans over rice. Add steamed broccoli, a salad, and a glass of wine, and I'm in gastronomic heaven. After dinner cleanup, we enjoy a walk around the neighborhood with our children. It's important to us to show our kids the importance we place on physical activity. And I don't have to be concerned about trying to get my formal exercise in because it's already done.

As night descends, I enjoy spending time with the family outside, pointing out some of the features of the night sky. There is plenty of fodder for storytelling, given the fanciful origins of the constellations in Greek mythology. Getting up at 4:30 A.M. also encourages a reasonable bedtime, and it eliminates the need for sleeping pills!

Did You Meet Your Goal?

So, what did you accomplish today? Did you take your scientific knowledge and put it to good use?

From what we've discussed in earlier chapters, it's clear that controlling your calories is very important. The next time you're out at a restaurant, take a look around. You'll probably see a number of elderly people, but if you notice—most are close to their ideal body weight. That old chestnut is true: "Little old ladies are old because they're little."

The day I described provided great-tasting meals and between-meal solutions when hunger comes calling. Fats weren't eliminated from the diet—both the Benecol spread and the salmon have a high fat content—but it's important to know which types of fat to eat. It is clear certain fats are quite heart-healthy, including the plant stanol esters of Benecol and the omega-3 fatty acids in salmon. Saturated fat, the heart-unhealthy fat, is very low in the diet described. Most importantly, my day restricted calories. This is the universal feature of diets that work.

We've already discussed the favorable impact of exercise; the day began embracing that knowledge with an enjoyable walking program.

Perhaps the most important thing to keep in mind in revamping your heart-healthy lifestyle is a sense of purpose. Regardless of your age and the extent of your medical difficulties, isn't there some friend or close family member who could benefit from seeing how you overcome your obstacles?

You now know the facts about CRP, inflammation, cholesterol, and lifestyle choices and how they impact our existence. You've been provided a template for success that you can customize for yourself.

I now challenge you to be a role model for others. You just might save your own life in the process!

Appendix A

Heart-Related Organizations

ARTHRITIS

Arthritis Foundation
P.O. Box 7669
Atlanta, GA 30357-0669
(800) 283-7800
www.arthritis.org

The only national nonprofit organization that supports the more than one hundred types of arthritis and related conditions with advocacy, programs, services, and research.

National Institute of Arthritis and Musculoskeletal and Skin Diseases
Information Clearinghouse
1 AMS Circle
Bethesda, MD 20892-3675
(877) 226-4267; (301) 495-4484 (Voice)
(301) 565-2966 (TTY)
www.niams.nih.gov

This federal institute supports research into the causes, treatment, and prevention of arthritis and musculoskeletal and skin diseases, the training of basic and clinical scientists to carry out this research, and the dissemination of information on research progress in these diseases.

DIABETES

American Diabetes Association
1660 Duke Street
Alexandria, VA 22314
(800) 232-3472; (703) 549-1500
www.diabetes.org

The nation's leading nonprofit health organization providing diabetes research, information, and advocacy. The ADA funds research, publishes scientific findings, provides information and other services to people with diabetes, their families, health care professionals, and the public, and advocates for scientific research and for the rights of people with diabetes.

National Diabetes Information Clearinghouse
One Information Way
Bethesda, MD 20892
(301) 654-3327
www.niddk.nih.gov

A service of the National Institute of Diabetes and Digestive and Kidney Diseases. Established in 1987, the clearinghouse provides information and research into the care and treatment of diabetes.

National Institute of Diabetes and Digestive and Kidney Diseases
Information Clearinghouse
3 Information Way
Bethesda, MD 20892
(301) 654-4415
www.niddk.nih.gov

This federal institute conducts and supports research on diabetes and many serious diseases affecting digestion and kidneys.

GENERAL GOVERNMENT ORGANIZATIONS

Centers for Disease Control and Prevention (CDC)
1600 Clifton Road
Atlanta, GA 30333
(404) 639-3534; (800) 311-3435
www.cdc.gov

The mission of the CDC is to promote health and quality of life by preventing and controlling disease, injury, and disability.

Food and Drug Administration (FDA)
5600 Fishers Lane
Rockville, MD 20857
(301) 472-4750
www.fda.gov

The FDA regulates drugs and medical devices to ensure that they are safe and effective. This government agency provides a number of publications for consumers.

National Institutes of Health (NIH)
Office of Communications and Public Liaison
Building 1, Room 344
1 Center Drive, MSC 0188
Bethesda, MD 20892-0188
(301) 496-4000
www.nih.gov

A federally funded medical research organization dedicated to preventing and treating disease. Cardiovascular disease research is conducted through the NIH National Heart, Lung and Blood Institute.

HEART PROBLEMS

American College of Cardiology
Heart House
9111 Old Georgetown Road
Bethesda, MD 20814-1699
(800) 253-4636
www.acc.org

This organization of more than twenty-five thousand cardiovascular scientists and physicians supports professional education, research, and quality standards and represents its membership in the development of and advocacy for public health care policy.

American Heart Association
7272 Greenville Avenue
Dallas, TX 75231
(800) 242-8721
www.americanheart.org

A nonprofit association trying to reduce disability and death from cardiovascular diseases and stroke and provide credible heart disease and stroke information for effective prevention and treatment.

American Society of Hypertension
515 Madison Avenue
New York, NY 10022
(212) 644-0650
www.ash-us.org

Founded in 1985, ASH is dedicated to the scientific investigation of high blood pressure. ASH organizes and conducts activities that promote and encourage research and the exchange of scientific information related to hypertension and heart disease.

Cardiac Arrhythmias Research and Education Foundation
2082 Michelson Drive, Suite 301
Irvine, CA 92612
(800) 404-9500
www.longqt.com

This foundation promotes public awareness of long QT syndrome and other cardiac arrhythmias and funds medical research in the areas of cardiac arrhythmias and sudden cardiac death.

InterAmerican Heart Foundation (IHF)
7272 Greenville Avenue
Dallas, TX 75231-4596
(214) 706-1218
www.iahf.org

The IHF promotes an awareness of heart disease and stroke risk and prevention throughout North, Central, and South America, as well as in the Caribbean. The IHF coordinates advocacy and education programs.

International Society on Hypertension in Blacks (ISHB)
2045 Manchester Street, NE
Atlanta, GA 30324
(404) 875-6263
www.ishib.org

Founded in 1986, the ISHB is committed to improving the health and lives of ethnic populations facing a high risk of high blood pressure. Activities include promoting research, community education, meetings, and publications.

National Cholesterol Education Program (NCEP)
NHLBI Health Information Network
P.O. Box 30105
Bethesda, MD 20824-0105
(301) 592-8573
www.nhlbi.nih.gov/about/ncep

A program of the National Heart, Lung and Blood Institute, the NCEP emphasizes public awareness of cholesterol as a major risk factor for coronary heart disease (CHD) and death and disease resulting from CHD.

National Heart Council
306 W. Joppa Road
Baltimore, MD 21204-4048
(800) 332-NEMA [(800-332-6362)]
www.nemahealth.org/aboutus.html

A program of the National Emergency Medicine Association to support NEMAs mission of promoting research and education in the fight against cardiovascular disease.

National Heart, Lung and Blood Institute
NHLBI Health Information Center
P.O. Box 30105
Bethesda, MD 20824-0105
(301) 592-8573
(240) 629-3255 (TTY)
www.nhlbi.nih.gov

The NHLBI provides leadership for a national program in diseases of the heart, blood vessels, lungs, and blood; blood resources; and sleep disorders. Since October 1997, the NHLBI has also had administrative responsibility for the NIH Women's Health Initiative.

WomenHeart
818 18th Street, NW, Suite 730
Washington, DC 20006
(202) 728-7199
www.womenheart.org

An information and advocacy group dedicated to providing facts about
women and heart disease and to decreasing death and disability among
women resulting from heart disease. The association offers print
materials, radio PSAs, support groups, a website, and a quarterly
newsletter.

World Heart Federation (WHF)
P.O. Box 117
CH-1211 Geneva 12, Switzerland
+00 41-22 347 67 55
www.worldheart.org

This consortium of cardiology and heart foundations from more than
seventy-five countries in the Americas, Asia-Pacific region, Europe, and
Africa is active in research, professional education, and public education.

LUPUS

Lupus Foundation of America, Inc.
1300 Piccard Drive, Suite 200
Rockville, MD 20850-4303
(301)670-9292
www.lupus.org

The only nationwide volunteer organization exclusively serving the
entire lupus community, including patients, their families, physicians,
researchers, and the general public. The mission is to educate and
support those affected by lupus and to find a cure. The LFA was
incorporated as a nonprofit health agency in 1977. Since its
establishment, the LFA has remained a grassroots, volunteer-driven
organization.

STROKE

American Stroke Association
7272 Greenville Avenue
Dallas, TX 75231
(888) 4STROKE
www.strokeassociation.org

A division of the American Heart Association, the ASA was formed in 1997 to promote information on warning signs, fund prevention research, work with physicians, and help stroke survivors and their families.

National Institute of Neurological Disorders and Stroke (NINDS)
Office of Communications and Public Liaison
Building 1, Room 344
1 Center Drive, MSC 0188
Bethesda, MD 20892-0188
(301-496-5924); (800) 352-9424
www.ninds.nih.gov

Associated with the National Institutes of Health, the NINDS promotes research toward prevention, diagnosis, and treatment of neurological disorders and stroke. The organization conducts its own research and provides funding and fellowships to others.

National Stroke Association (NSA)
9707 E. Easter Lane
Englewood, CO 80112-3747
(800) STROKES [(800) 787-6537]
www.stroke.org

The NSA is dedicated to professional and public issues related to all aspects of stroke treatment, rehabilitation, and prevention. Programs and activities are geared toward professional and patient education as well as family support.

WEIGHT CONTROL

American Obesity Association (AOA)
1250 24th Street, NW, Suite 300
Washington, DC 20037
(800) 98-OBESE [(800) 986-2373]
www.obesity.org

This association supports activities that further obesity research, raise public and professional awareness of obesity issues, and advocate for federal policies associated with this widespread problem.

Weight-Control Information Network
1 Win Way
Bethesda, MD 20892-3665
(301) 984-7378; or (800) WIN-8098
www.niddk.nih.gov/health/nutrit/win.htm

WIN is a national information service of the National Institute of Diabetes and Digestive and Kidney Diseases (NIDDK) established in 1994 to provide science-based information on obesity, weight control, and nutrition. WIN has also developed the Sisters Together: Move More, Eat Better Media program that encourages black women eighteen and over to maintain a healthy weight by becoming more physically active and eating healthier foods. WIN produces, collects, and disseminates materials on obesity, weight control, and nutrition.

WOMEN'S ISSUES

National Women's Health Resource Center (NWHRC)
120 Albany Street, Suite 820
New Brunswick, NJ 08901
(877) 986-9472
www.healthywomen.org

An independent, consumer-oriented not-for-profit organization founded in 1988 to focus on disease prevention and wellness for women. The NWHRC delivers information on a wide range of women's health issues, including heart-related conditions.

WomenHeart
818 18th Street, NW Suite 730
Washington, DC 20006
(202) 728-7199
www.womenheart.org

An information and advocacy group dedicated to providing facts about
women and heart disease and to decreasing death and disability among
women resulting from heart disease. The association offers print
materials, radio PSAs, support groups, a website, and a quarterly
newsletter.

Appendix B

Tips for Taking Your Own Blood Pressure

Your blood pressure isn't static; it changes all the time, depending on whether you're talking, moving, lying down, or standing up. With more and more people investing in their own blood pressure monitoring devices, here are a few tips to get an accurate reading:

- Don't smoke or drink caffeinated beverages at least thirty minutes before taking your blood pressure.
- Sit for five minutes with your feet flat on the floor before the test.
- Rest your arm on a table, at the level of your heart.
- Wear short sleeves to expose your arm (if you're using an arm cuff).
- Don't talk, laugh, or chew gum during the test.
- Take two readings two minutes apart, and average the results.
- If the two readings differ by more than 5 mm/Hg, do another set of two readings.

Appendix C

Lipid Profile Measurements

CHOLESTEROL

Your liver produces about 1,000 milligrams a day of cholesterol from saturated fat and another 400 to 500 milligrams from other foods you eat. You need some cholesterol, but too much can lead to artery disease. For every 10 mg/dl increase in HDL, you'll slash your heart attack risk in half.

Total Cholesterol

Desirable: less than 200 mg/dl
Borderline high risk: 200 to 239 mg/dl
High risk: 240 mg/dl and higher

LDL Cholesterol Level

The lower your LDL cholesterol, the lower your risk of heart disease (it's a better gauge of risk than total blood cholesterol).

Optimal: less than 100 mg/dl
Close to optimal: 100 to 129 mg/dl
Borderline high: 130 to 159 mg/dl
High: 160 to 189 mg/dl
Very high: 190 mg/dl and higher

HDL Cholesterol Level

HDL is the "good" cholesterol, so the more of it you have, the better.

Average healthy range (men): 40 to 50 mg/dl
Average healthy range (women): 50 to 60 mg/dl
Dangerously low: less than 40 mg/dl

TRIGLYCERIDE LEVEL

Normal: less than 150 mg/dl
Borderline high: 150 to 199 mg/dl
High: 200 to 499 mg/dl
Very high: 500 mg/dl and higher

Glossary

aneurysm A weak area on an artery that has ballooned out from the wall and filled with blood.

angina Heart pain caused by a shortage of blood and oxygen.

angioplasty A procedure in which a device with a small balloon on the tip of a catheter is inserted into a blood vessel to open up an area of blockage.

anticoagulant A drug used to prevent the formation of blood clots.

antigen A substance recognized as foreign by the immune system.

aorta The main artery of the body into which the heart pumps.

arrhythmia An abnormal heart rhythm.

arteriogram Also called an angiogram, an x-ray of the arteries and veins that uses a special dye that can detect blockage or narrowing of the vessels.

arteriosclerosis A general term for the hardening and thickening of the arterial walls.

artery Any of a number of blood vessels that carries blood from the heart to other parts of the body.

atheroma The fat deposits inside diseased arteries.

atherosclerosis A type of arteriosclerosis in which the artery walls thicken and narrow owing to the buildup of cholesterol in the inner layer of an artery, restricting blood flow and leading to a heart attack or stroke.

atrial fibrillation Irregular beating of the left upper chamber of the heart when electrical signals are fired in a rapid and uncontrolled manner.

atrium One of the heart's chambers that receives blood directly from a vein.

capillary Any of the tiny, thin-walled tubes that carry blood between arteries and veins.

cardiac arrest A condition in which the heart stops beating.

cardiac catheterization An examination of the heart by threading a thin tube into a vein or artery and passing it into the heart to sample oxygen levels, measure pressure, or take an x-ray.

cardiac perfusion imaging A noninvasive diagnostic procedure in which a radioactive tracer is injected into the bloodstream and collects in the wall of the heart. This test is used to assess the heart's blood flow or heart attack damage.

cardiomyopathy A disease of the heart muscle in which the heart loses its ability to pump blood; it may lead to disturbed heart rhythm and irregular heartbeats.

cardiovascular disease (CVD) Any abnormal condition of the heart or blood vessels, including coronary artery disease, stroke, congestive heart failure, peripheral vascular disease, congenital heart disease, and endocarditis.

carotid artery The artery on either side of the neck that supplies the brain with blood.

carotid endarterectomy Surgery used to remove fatty deposits from the carotid arteries.

cholesterol A waxy substance produced naturally by the liver that circulates in the blood and helps maintain tissues and cell membranes. Cholesterol is found throughout the body, including the nervous system, muscles, skin, liver, intestines, and heart. Too much cholesterol can contribute to atherosclerosis and high blood pressure.

congestive heart failure The inability of the heart to deliver adequate blood flow because of heart disease or high blood pressure. When this occurs, blood backs up into the veins leading to the heart, causing breathlessness, salt and water retention, and swelling.

coronary artery Either of two arteries that travel from the aorta over the top of the heart, providing blood to the heart.

coronary artery disease (CAD) Also known as ischemic heart disease, a condition caused by narrowed coronary arteries (atherosclerosis) that decrease the supply of blood to the heart (myocardial ischemia).

diabetes A condition in which there is not enough available insulin and the urine and blood contain excess sugar.

diaphragm The dome-shaped muscle located at the bottom of the lungs and used in breathing.

diastolic blood pressure The lower number in a blood pressure reading which represents the pressure inside the arteries when the heart is filling up with blood between contractions.

diuretic A medication that increases the rate that urine is produced, promoting the excretion of salts and water.

echocardiography A diagnostic technique that uses ultrasound waves and that may be performed while the patient is either resting or exercising.

electrocardiogram (EKG) A type of cardiovascular test that records the electrical impulses produced by the heart.

enzyme A protein that causes or speeds up a chemical reaction in the body. Enzymes help synthesize most compounds in the body.

fibrin A white protein that helps form blood clots.

free radical A toxic chemical released during the process of cellular respiration and released in excessive amounts as a cell dies.

heart attack An acute condition that occurs when a section of the heart doesn't get enough oxygenated blood and dies. A heart attack is caused by blockage of one or more of the coronary arteries.

high-density lipoprotein (HDL) So-called good cholesterol, containing mostly protein and less cholesterol and triglyceride. High levels are associated with lower risk of coronary artery disease.

homocysteine An amino acid that occurs normally in the body. In high levels, homocysteine may increase a person's chances of developing heart disease and stroke.

hypertension The medical term for high blood pressure.

infarct An area of tissue that is dead or dying because of a loss of blood supply.

ischemia Decline in blood supply.

lipid Any of various fatty substances (including cholesterol and triglycerides) found in blood and tissues.

low-density lipoprotein (LDL) So-called bad cholesterol. High levels are associated with increased risk of coronary artery disease.

myocardial infarction Heart attack.

myocardial ischemia Lack of oxygen-carrying blood in an area of heart tissue due to blocked coronary arteries. Myocardial ischemia can cause chest pain, but it also can be painless. Without intervention, myocardial ischemia can lead to a heart attack.

oxidizing Combining chemically with oxygen.

pacemaker An electrical device that controls the heartbeat and heart rhythm by emitting a series of electrical charges.

peripheral arterial disease (PAD) A condition causing poor circulation in the legs that (when untreated) increases the risk of heart attack, stroke, amputation, and death.

plaque The buildup of fatty substances, cholesterol, cellular waste products, calcium, and fibrin (a clotting material in the blood) in the inner lining of an artery.

platelet A colorless, disk-shaped body in blood that aids in blood clotting.

protein An amino acid compound that the body uses for growth and repair. Foods that supply the body with protein include animal products, grains, legumes, and vegetables.

pulmonary artery One of the arteries carrying deoxygenated blood from the heart to the lungs.

stent A tiny, expandable coil that is placed inside a blood vessel at the site of a blockage and then expanded to open up the blockage.

stroke Loss of muscle function, vision, sensation, or speech caused by either a hemorrhage or an insufficient supply of blood to part of the brain, often due to narrowing of the arteries supplying blood to the brain. The hemorrhage may involve bleeding into the brain itself or into the space around the brain.

systolic blood pressure The top number in a blood pressure reading, which is a measure of the pressure inside the arteries as the heart contracts.

total serum cholesterol A combined measurement of a person's high-density lipoprotein (HDL) and low-density lipoprotein (LDL).

triglyceride A type of fat carried through the bloodstream to tissues. Most of the body's fat tissue is stored in the form of triglycerides for later use. Triglycerides are obtained primarily from fats in foods.

unsaturated fat A type of fat that is usually liquid at refrigerator temperature. Monounsaturated fat and polyunsaturated fat are two kinds of unsaturated fat.

valve An opening between two chambers of the heart or between a heart chamber and a blood vessel. When a heart valve is closed, no blood should leak through.

ventricle One of the two lower heart chambers.

ventricular fibrillation Electrical signals in the ventricles that are fired in a rapid and uncontrolled manner, causing the heart to quiver rather than beat and pump blood.

Bibliography

Abramson J. L., and V. Vaccarino. "Relationship Between Physical Activity and Inflammation Among Apparently Healthy Middle-Aged and Older U.S. Adults." *Archives of Internal Medicine* 162 (2002): 1286–92.

AHA Scientific Statement. "Fish Consumption, Fish Oil, Omega-3 Fatty Acids and Cardiovascular Disease, #71-0241." *Circulation* 106 (2002): 2747–57.

———. "AHA Dietary Guidelines: Revision 2000, #71-0193." *Circulation* 102 (2000): 2284–99.

Albert, C. M., et al. "Prospective Study of C-Reactive Protein, Homocysteine, and Plasma Lipid Levels As Predictors of Sudden Cardiac Death," *Circulation* 105 (2002): 2595–99.

Bazzino, O., et al. "C-Reactive Protein, and the Stress Tests for the Risk Stratification of Patients Recovering from Unstable Angina Pectoris." *American Journal of Cardiology* 87, 11 (2001): 1235–39.

Berk, B. C., W. S. Weintraub, and R. W. Alexander. "Elevation of C-Reactive Protein in 'Active' Coronary Artery Disease." *American Journal of Cardiology* 65 (1990): 168–72

Bermudez, E. A., and P. M. Ridker. "C-Reactive Protein, Statins, and the Primary Prevention of Atherosclerotic Cardiovascular Disease." *Preventive Cardiology* 5 (2002): 42–46.

Black, Henry R., et al. "Principal Results of the Controlled Onset Verapamil Investigation of Cardiovascular End Points (CONVINCE) Trial." *Journal of the American Medical Association* 289 (2003): 2073–82.

Buffn, A., et al. "Widespread Coronary Inflammation in Unstable Angina." *New England Journal of Medicine* 347 (2002): 5–12.

Casscells, W., M. Naghavi, and J. T. Willerson. "Vulnerable Atherosclerotic Plaque: A Multifocal Disease." *Circulation* 107 (2003): 2072–75

Chan, A. W., et al. "Relation of Inflammation and Benefit of Statins After Percutaneous Coronary Interventions." *Circulation* 107 (2003): 1750–56.

Chung M. K., et al. "C-Reactive Protein Elevation in Patients with Atrial Arrhythmias: Inflammatory Mechanisms and Persistence of Atrial Fibrillation." *Circulation* 104 (2001): 2886–91.

Cushman, M., et al. "Effect of Postmenopausal Hormones on Inflammation-Sensitive Proteins: The Postmenopausal Estrogen-Progestin Interventions (PEPI) Study." *Circulation* 100 (1999): 717–22.

Danesh, J., et al. "Low Grade Inflammation and Coronary Heart Disease: Prospective Study and Updated Meta-Analyses." *British Medical Journal* 321 (2001): 199–204.

Engeli, S., et al. "Association Between Adiponectin and Mediators of Inflammation in Obese Women." *Diabetes* 52 (2003): 942–47.

Ewart, H. K. M. "Absence of Diurnal Variation of C-Reactive Protein Levels in Healthy Human Subjects." *Clinical Chemistry* 47 (2001): 426–30.

Fade, A. M., and N. I. Rivera. "The Role of C-Reactive Protein As a Prognostic Indicator in Advanced Cancer." *Current Oncology Reports* 4 (May 1, 2002): 250–55.

Ford, E. S., and W. H. Giles. "Serum C-Reactive Protein and Self-Reported Stroke: Findings from the Third National Health and Nutrition Examination Survey." *Arteriosclerosis Thrombosis and Vascular Biology* 20 (2000): 1052–56.

Fuster, V., et al. "Aspirin As a Therapeutic Agent in Cardiovascular Disease." *Circulation* 87 (1993): 659–75.

Genest, J., and T. R. Pedersen. "Prevention of Cardiovascular Ischemic Events: High-Risk and Secondary Prevention." *Circulation* 107 (2003): 2059–65

Grady, D., et al. "Cardiovascular Disease Outcomes During 6.8 Years of Hormone Therapy: Heart and Estrogen/Progestin Replacement Study Follow-Up (HERS II)." *Journal of the American Medical Association* 288 (2002): 49–57.

Grodstein, F., et al. "Understanding the Divergent Data on Postmenopausal Hormone Therapy." *New England Journal of Medicine* 348 (2003): 645–50.

Grundy, S. M., et al. "Cardiovascular Risk Assessment Based on U.S. Cohort Studies: Findings from a National Heart, Lung and Blood Institute Workshop." *Circulation* 104 (2001): 491–96.

Guzzetti, S., G. Costantino, and C. Fundaro. "Systemic Inflammation, Atrial Fibrillation, and Cancer." *Circulation* 106, 9 (August 27, 2002): e40.

Hanley J. A., and B. J. McNeil. "The Meaning and Use of the Area Under a Receiver Operating Characteristic (ROC) Curve." Abstract. *Radiology* 143 (1982): 29–36.

Haverkate, F., et al. "Production of C-Reactive Protein and Risk of Coronary Events in Stable and Unstable Angina." European Concerted Action on Thrombosis and Disabilities Angina Pectoris Study Group. *The Lancet* 349 (1997): 462–66.

Heart Protection Study Collaborative Group. "MRC/BHF Heart Protection Study of Cholesterol Lowering with Simvastatin in 20,536 High-Risk Individuals: A Randomised Placebo-Controlled Trial." *The Lancet* 360 (2002): 7–22.

Hennekens, C. H., M. A. Jonas, and J. E. Buring. "The Benefits of Aspirin in Acute Myocardial Infarction: Still a Well-Kept Secret in the U.S." *Archives of Internal Medicine* 154 (1994): 37–39.

Imhof, A., et al. "Effect of Alcohol Consumption on Systemic Markers of Inflammation." *The Lancet* 357 (2001): 763–67.

Keaney, J. F., and J. A. Vita. "The Value of Inflammation for Predicting Unstable Angina." *New England Journal of Medicine* 347 (2002): 55–57.

Khairy, P., et al. "Absence of Association Between Infectious Agents and Endothelial Function in Healthy Young Men." *Circulation* 107 (2003): 1966–71.

King, D. E., et al. "C-Reactive Protein and Glycemic Control in Adults with Diabetes," *Diabetes Care* 26 (2003): 1535–39.

Koenig, W. "C-Reactive Protein and Cardiovascular Risk: Has the Time Come for Screening the General Population?" *Clinical Chemistry* 47, 1 (2001): 9–10.

Koenig, W., et al. "C-Reactive Protein, a Sensitive Marker of Inflammation, Predicts Future Risk of Coronary Heart Disease in Initially Healthy Middle-Aged Men: Results from the MONICA (Monitoring Trends and Determinants in Cardiovascular Disease) Augsburg Cohort Study, 1984 to 1992." *Circulation* 99 (1999): 237–42.

Kushner, I., and A. R. Sehgal. "Is High-Sensitivity C-Reactive Protein an Effective Screening Test for Cardiovascular Risk?" *Archives of Internal Medicine* 162 (2002): 867–69.

LaMonte, M. J., et al. "Cardiorespiratory Fitness and C-Reactive Protein Among Tri-Ethnic Sample of Women." *Circulation* 106 (2002): 403–6.

Libby, P., P. M. Ridker, and A. Maseri. "Inflammation and Atherosclerosis." *Circulation* 105 (2002): 1135–43.

Liuzzo, G., et al. "The Prognosis Value of C-Reactive Protein and Serum Amyloid Protein in Severe Unstable Angina," *New England Journal of Medicine* 331 (1994): 417–24.

Lloyd-Jones, D. M., et al. "C-Reactive Protein in the Prediction of Cardiovascular Events." *New England Journal of Medicine* 348 (2003): 1059–61.

Mascitelli, L., and F. Pezzetta. "Lipid-Lowering Therapy and Risk of Coronary Events." *Journal of the American Medical Association* 289 (2003): 2071.

McMillan, D. C., K. Canna, and C. S. McArdle. "Systemic Inflammatory Response Predicts Survival Following Curative Resection of Colorectal Cancer." *British Journal of Surgery* 90, 2 (February 2003): 215–19.

McMillan, D. C., et al. "Measurement of the Systemic Inflammatory Response Predicts Cancer-Specific and Non-Cancer Survival in Patients with Cancer." *Nutrition and Cancer* 41, 1–2 (2001): 64–69.

Mortensen, R. F., and A. B. Rudczynski. "Prognostic Significance of Serum CRP Levels and Lymphoid Cell Infiltrates in Human Breast Cancer." *Oncology* 19, 3 (1982): 129–33.

Mosca, L. "C-Reactive Protein—To Screen or Not to Screen?" *New England Journal of Medicine* 347 (2002): 1615–17.

Mosca, L., et al. "Hormone Replacement Therapy and Cardiovascular Disease: A Statement for Healthcare Professionals from the American Heart Association." *Circulation* 104 (2001): 499–503.

Nozoe, T. "Significance of Preoperative Elevation of Serum C-Reactive Protein As an Indicator for Prognosis in Colorectal Cancer." *American Journal of Surgery* 176, 4 (October 1998): 335–38

Nozoe T., et al. "Immunohistochemical Expression of C-Reactive Protein in Squamous Cell Carcinoma of the Esophagus—Significance As a Tumor Marker." *Cancer Letters* 192, 1 (March 20, 2003): 89–95.

Nozoe T., et al. "Preoperative Elevation of Serum C-Reactive Protein Is Related to Impaired Immunity in Patients with Colorectal Cancer." *American Journal of Clinical Oncology* 23, 3 (June 2000): 263-6.

Ockene, I. S, et al. "Variability and Classification Accuracy of Serial High-Sensitivity C-Reactive Protein Measurements in Healthy Adults." *Clinical Chemistry* 47 (2001): 444–50.

Pearson, T. A., et al. "Markers of Inflammation and Cardiovascular Disease: Application to Clinical and Public Health Practice: A Statement for Healthcare Professionals from the Centers for Disease Control and

Prevention and the American Heart Association. *Circulation* 107 (2003): 499–511.

Pepys, M. B., and G. M. Hirschfield. "C-Reactive Protein: A Critical Update." *Journal of Clinical Investigation* 111, 12 (June 2003): 1805–12.

Pradhan, A. D., et al. "C-Reactive Protein, Interleukin 6, and Risk of Developing Type 2 Diabetes Mellitus." *Journal of the American Medical Association* 286 (2001): 327–34.

Pradhan, A. D., et al. "Inflammatory Biomarkers, Hormone Replacement Therapy, and Incident Coronary Heart Disease: Prospective Analysis from the Women's Health Initiative Observational Study." *Journal of the American Medical Association* 288 (2002): 980–87.

Reynolds, T. M., P. Twomey, and A. S. Wierzbicki. "Accuracy of Cardiovascular Risk Estimation." *Clinical Chemistry* 49 (2003): 706–7.

Ridker P. M., "Clinical Application of C-Reactive Protein for Cardiovascular Disease Detection and Prevention." *Circulation* 107 (2003): 363–69.

———. "High Sensitivity C-Reactive Protein. Potential Adjunct for Global Risk Assessment in the Primary Prevention of Cardiovascular Disease," *Circulation* (2001): 1813–18.

Ridker, P. M., and N. Rifai. "High Sensitivity C-Reactive Protein: A Novel and Promising Marker of Coronary Heart Disease." *Clinical Chemistry* 47, 3 (2001): 403–11.

Ridker P. M., R. J. Glynn, and C. H. Hennekens. "C-Reactive Protein Adds to the Predictive Value of Total and HDL Cholesterol in Determining Risk of First Myocardial Infarction." *Circulation* 97 (1998): 2007–11.

Ridker, P. M., M. J. Stampfer, and N. Rifai. "Novel Risk Factors for Systemic Atherosclerosis: A Comparison of C-Reactive Protein, Fibrinogen, Homocysteine, Lipoprotein(a), and Standard Cholesterol Screening as Predictors of Peripheral Arterial Disease." *Journal of the American Medical Association* 285 (2001): 2481–85.

Ridker, P. M., et al. "Comparison of C-Reactive Protein and Low-Density Lipoprotein Cholesterol Levels in the Prediction of First Cardiovascular Events." *New England Journal of Medicine* 347, 20 (November 14 2002): 1557–65.

Ridker, P. M., et al. "C-Reactive Protein and Other Markers of Inflammation in the Prediction of Cardiovascular Disease in Women." *New England Journal of Medicine* 342 (2000): 836–43.

Ridker, P. M., et al. "Hormone Replacement Therapy and Increased Plasma Concentration of C-Reactive Protein." *Circulation* 100 (1999): 713–16.

Ridker, P. M., et al. "Inflammation, Aspirin, and the Risk of Cardiovascular Disease in Apparently Healthy Men." *New England Journal of Medicine* 336 (1997): 973–79.

Ridker, P. M. et al. "Measurement of C-Reactive Protein for the Targeting of Statin Therapy in the Primary Prevention of Acute Coronary Events." *New England Journal of Medicine* 344 (2001): 1959–65.

Rifai, N., and P. M. Ridker. "Population Distributions of C-Reactive Protein in Apparently Healthy Men and Women in the United States: Implication for Clinical Interpretation." *Clinical Chemistry* 49 (2001): 666–69.

———. "Proposed Cardiovascular Risk Assessment Algorithm Using High-Sensitivity C-Reactive Protein and Lipid Screen." *Clinical Chemistry* 47, 1 (2001): 28–30.

Rifai, N., et al. "Is C-Reactive Protein Specific for Vascular Disease in Women?" *Annals of Internal Medicine* 136 (2002): 529–33.

Riggs, B. L., and L. C. Hartmann. "Selective Estrogen-Receptor Modulators—Mechanisms of Action and Application to Clinical Practice." *New England Journal of Medicine* 348 (2003): 618–29.

Roberts, W. L., et al. "Evaluation of Nine Automated High-Sensitivity C-Reactive Protein Methods: Implications for Clinical and Epidemiological Applications." *Clinical Chemistry* 47 (2001): 418–25. [Erratum: *Clinical Chemistry* 47 (2001): 980.]

Ross, R. "Atherosclerosis—An Inflammatory Disease." *New England Journal of Medicine* 340 (1999): 115–26.

Rost, N. S., et al. "Plasma Concentration of C-Reactive Protein and Risk of Ischemic Stroke and Transient Ischemic Attack: The Framingham Study." *Stroke* 32 (2001): 2575–79.

Sharma, A. M., et al. "Effects of Exercise on Plasma Lipoproteins." *New England Journal of Medicine* 348 (2003): 1494–96.

Spence, J. D., and J. Norris. "Infection, Inflammation, and Atherosclerosis." *Stroke* 34 (2003): 333–34.

Stewart, S. H., A. G. Mainous, and G. Gilbert. "Relation Between Alcohol Consumption and C-Reactive Protein Levels in the Adult U.S. Population." *Journal of the American Board of Family Practice* 15 (2002): 437–42.

Szalai, A. J., et al. "Association Between Baseline Levels of C-Reactive Protein (CRP) and a Dinucleotide Repeat Polymorphism in the Intron of the CRP Gene." *Genes and Immunity* 3 (2002): 14–19.

Tiemeier, H., et al. "Plasma Fatty Acid Composition and Depression Are Associated in the Elderly: The Rotterdam Study." *American Journal of Clinical Nutrition* 78, 1 (July): 40–46.

Tracy, R. P., et al. "Relationship of C-Reactive Protein to Risk of Cardiovascular Disease in the Elderly: Results from the Cardiovascular Health Study and the Rural Health Promotion Project." *Arteriosclerosis Thrombosis and Vascular Biology* 17 (1997): 1121–27.

Vakkilainen, J., et al. "Relationships Between Low-Density Lipoprotein Particle Size, Plasma Lipoproteins, and Progression of Coronary Artery Disease: The Diabetes Atherosclerosis Intervention Study (DAIS)." *Circulation* 107 (2003): 1733–37.

Vongpatanasin, W., et al. "Differential Effects of Oral Versus Transdermal Estrogen Replacement Therapy on C-Reactive Protein in Postmenopausal Women." *Journal of the American College of Cardiology* 41, 8 (April 16, 2003): 1358–63.

Wang, C.-H., et al. "C-Reactive Protein Upregulates Angiotensin Type 1 Receptors in Vascular Smooth Muscle." *Circulation* 107 (2003): 1783–90.

Wilson, P. W. F., et al. "Prediction of Coronary Heart Disease Using Risk Factor Categories." *Circulation* 97 (1998): 1837–47.

Writing Group for the Women's Health Initiative Investigators. "Risks and Benefits of Estrogen Plus Progestin in Healthy Postmenopausal Women: Principal Results from the Women's Health Initiative Randomized Controlled Trial." *Journal of the American Medical Association* 288 (2002): 321–33.

Yeh, E., and J. T. Willerson. "Coming of Age of C-Reactive Protein: Using Inflammation Markers in Cardiology." *Circulation* 107 (2003): 370–71.

Yu, H, and N. Rifai. "High-Sensitivity C-Reactive Protein and Atherosclerosis: From Theory to Therapy." *Clinical Biochemistry* 33 (2000): 601–10.

Zimmerman, M. A., et al. "Diagnostic Implications of C-Reactive Protein." *Archives of Surgery* 138 (2003): 220–24.

Index